D1446864

Every Mary Needs an Elizabeth

*Divine Relationships for a Reason,
A Season, or a Lifetime*

Dr. Karene Joye Keane

Copyright © 2019 Karene Joye Keane

All rights reserved

No part of this book may be reproduced, or stored in a retrieval system, or transmitted in any form or by any means, electronic, mechanical, photocopying, recording, or otherwise, without express written permission of the publisher.

ISBN-9798642315590

Printed in the United States of America
First Printing 2021

K. Joye Keane
P.O. Box 1149 Reading
Montego Bay, St. James, Jamaica

Email: church@fcotr.com
876-940-0298

Contents

Foreword

It is a wondrous gift from God when He brings two women from different races, countries and cultures together into a Holy Spirit inspired and connected friendship. Joye Keane and I have had such a divinely appointed relationship over the last two decades. I am honoured to write the forward for Every Mary Needs an Elizabeth. Joye has lived every Word of this book, creating an authentic work of integrity and truth. It is a message birthed from raw experience. Joye, more than any other woman I know, has totally surrendered to the will and purpose of God in and through her. She has done this in the face of repeated, seemingly insurmountable challenges with an indomitable spirit. Defeat is not in her vocabulary. The Word of God dwells in her richly and is reflected in every chapter. The hard-fought lessons she has accumulated are wise counsel for all women; we cannot do life alone. God has strategically placed other women in our lives for our spiritual growth and health. We can be victorious in every circumstance of life with the acknowledgment and acceptance of each "Elizabeth" God appoints along our journey. With enthusiastic confidence, I encourage every woman to read and embrace Joye's lessons in Every Mary Needs an Elizabeth.

Rev. Mary Holland

This book is dedicated to

My sister, Denver Marie Keane. You were
my Elizabeth...The Reason

My friend, Gillian Kaye Bahlai. You made a Dream
that started with a Thought a Reality... The Season

To my 1st born, Jean-Ann Karene Murray, the Mary in my
journey. These writings are dedicated to you for you have lived this "Life
giving journey of relationship". Thank you for taking on this project of
editing and re-editing and illustrating, making this my Dream come true.

I have waited.....

....A Lifetime

Introduction

"If anyone should ever write my life story, for whatever reason there might be, you'll be there between every line of pain and glory, cause you're the best thing that ever happened to me."
GLADYS KNIGHT

The Beauty of a Woman

"The beauty of a woman is not in the clothes she wears; neither is it in the figure she carries, nor the way she combs her hair. The beauty of a woman is not in a well-placed facial mole. True beauty is reflected in a woman's soul. It must be seen from her eyes because that is the doorway to her heart, the place where love resides. It is the passionate caring she lovingly gives. This kind of beauty keeps growing with passing years, never diminishing."
AUDREY HEPBURN

This book was conceived a long time ago and has been developing over years as I have lived out its powerful messages. Because our times are in the Master's hands, now is the time for its birth. Proverbs 17:17 tells us *"a friend loves at all times and a brother is there for adversity, but there is one who sticks closer than a brother."*

Every Mary Needs an Elizabeth is about these life-giving relationships.

I have had many opportunities to live among and spend quality time with some very precious women. Each of these women of

God allowed me to enter a magnificent relationship that daily evolved into the heavenly with Jesus. My life has never been the same because of them. I thank them for lovingly pouring into my life so that I could recognize that "correction is not rejection, but protection and direction." (Jim Frease)

Family members and friends continually provide life-giving relationships at strategic intervals of life's journey. They take us to high fun times and carry us through some low sad times. We share the most intimate hours sitting in silence with the joy of knowing we are not alone. That is heavenly. Most cherished are those times when we have listened instead of spoken, gaining so much more than the opposite would have provided.

My own experiences and journey have taken me through fun times, war times, and misunderstood times. There have been times of rejections and many occasions for sadness. I have had times of sharing the most intimate hours, and others when I have been forced to make the decision of peace myself as I moved from one time or season to another. I have spent hours of endless enquiries to God because of disappointments or heart-rending issues. At the time they made no sense to me. There were some forgettable experiences along the way, Selah!

Embracing children has provided so much excitement, both expected and unexpected! Being pregnant or wanting to be pregnant. The sharing and caring backed up learning more to share and care, and graciously provided those invaluable instructions so I could "do it right." Wow!

In all that has been said; every twist, turn, mishap, and victory has been used to shape me. They were pivotal at different junctions and crossroads in my life and ministry, vital and incredible help in taking my stand.

Every Mary Needs an Elizabeth. I identified my Elizabeth. I have had my Elizabeth's – actually several. I have also been a Mary several times over as I experienced my season. I honour the Mary's, the mentees, and Elizabeth's, the mentors, in my life. Some came for a season and others came into my life for a reason. A few will actually be with me for a lifetime. I thank God for each one who taught me that I, too, could become an Elizabeth to a Mary. This revelation is the dearest and most treasured legacy – I can be both, and so can you!

This book has been in the spiritual realm since 1999. My Heavenly Father and I spoke about it. We agreed on the topic. It has been written! Today you have finally gotten around to reading it, then, like myself, you have been in either the preparation phase or transition. This is your time to discover Every Mary Needs an Elizabeth. Everybody needs somebody. No one wants to be alone. Human nature is always seeking better because we are all people of passion and destiny seeking. We are all created as throne gazers with heaven's calling.

God supernaturally causes our paths to be crossed by various personalities – characters in different styles and makeup. Many will come. You must discern and determine if they are there for a reason, a season, or those God has sent to be there for a lifetime.

$\mathcal{P}$rologue

Reasons And Seasons

Life is a journey, and the pathway of each life can bring glory to God. Obviously, the outcome has a lot to do with how connected we are to the One who made us and who holds the blue print for our lives. The outcomes encompass Jeremiah 29:11; *for the plans I have for you are for good; to give you a hope and a future, an expected end.*

Some individuals are very calloused about relationships, even friendships. "It is what it is," They say. "You cannot trust people. They use you and abuse you, and sometimes leave you for dead." Here are a few more frequently heard phrases: you win some, you lose some; people come, and people go; you can only depend upon yourself. Whatever the outcome, you learn from it, then laugh at it, and eventually let it go. When it comes to relationships and friendships, I take it a bit further. Some of us, believing it is out of our hands, still try to manipulate. We make powerless attempts to chart a course that bears no fruit and leaves us feeling ashamed, condemned, and frustrated.

Our inability to choose properly is really the issue. We can get a lot of counsel after we have made a mess. We can read books on how to make friends and influence people. I believe we do hold the keys to relationships, but only One knows our future and expected end. That is God, our Father and Maker. I am a convert of simply submitting to God, and I constantly rehearse those life-changing words as Mary spoke, *"Be it unto me according to your*

Word."

As life goes, it is always difficult to choose the right friends all the time. Hence, we must categorize; reason, season, or lifetime. I have found this to be a safe harbor. Who was Mary? What did she know, and why did she choose Elizabeth to whom to run? These are "meaning to life" questions.

The life of the Messiah was given to Mary to both carry and protect. She was the handmaiden of the Lord, the carrier of the anointing. Her praise was directed to God as she told the story of her life, present and future – *"for the Lord took notice of his lowly servant."* Luke 1:46 TLB. I would submit to you that the reason Mary went to Elizabeth was that Elizabeth was already equipped with what Mary needed to help her with this journey. She sought out Elizabeth, a woman who could enter into her passion. In fact, the anointing on Mary and on the child she carried was so strong that the unborn child in Elizabeth's womb leaped within her as they approached. Elizabeth was carrying the promise of the "one crying in the wilderness," the one who was the path finder in preparation for the arrival of the King of Kings. Elizabeth was able to relate to the miracle of this immaculate conception.

Mary was carrying the world's Deliverer from sin. Here was the meaning into her life. What are you carrying? Don't we have the same life of Jesus on the inside of us? Are we not carriers of the same anointing Mary carried? Shouldn't we have the same effect on those of the same faith and fellow carriers of this anointing?

I have been profoundly inspired by this amazing account of Elizabeth's response to Mary in Luke 1:41; *At the sound of your voice the baby leaped in my womb.* Mary loved God and found favour with Him. She was chosen to bear the Messiah, the King of Kings and Lord of Lords, the conquering Lion of the Tribe of Judah.

How beautiful was that song that Mary sang as the anointing flowed through her, declaring and prophesying those profound lines from Luke 1: 46-55?

My soul magnifies the Lord,

And my spirit has rejoiced in God my Savior.

For He has regarded the lowly state of His maidservant;

For behold, henceforth all generations will call me blessed.

For He who is mighty has done great things for me,

And holy is His name.

And His mercy is on those who fear Him

From generation to generation.

He has shown strength with His arm;

He has scattered the proud in the imagination of their hearts.

He has put down the mighty from their thrones,

And exalted the lowly.

He has filled the hungry with good things,

And the rich He has sent away empty.

He has helped His servant Israel,

In remembrance of His mercy,

As He spoke to our fathers,

To Abraham and to his seed forever." NKJV

This was an appointed time. These two women were valuable to the kingdom of God! There was a great call on their lives to walk in a greater level of anointing and influence. How glorious was their call to give birth to and nurture the future that was imminent on the nation of Israel. It was the invasion of heaven coming to earth. Elizabeth would give birth to a son whose name would be miraculously declared John by his father Zechariah's supernaturally muted tongue. This John would be known throughout history as John the Baptist, the forerunner of the Messiah. Mary would give birth to Emmanuel, Jesus Christ of Nazareth, the Messiah, the Saviour of the world, who would save men from their sin. Elizabeth was positioned by God to fulfill the "reason" phase of Mary's charted journey.

Everybody needs somebody; no one wants to be alone. Human nature is always seeking better relationships, better meaningful fellowship. Why? Because we all have a deep desire for authenticity and passion to fulfill our destinies in the earth. It is in our DNA.

It's worthy of profound note that Mary stayed with Elizabeth for three months, yet beyond that she is not mentioned in the Bible. Her presence applied to the destiny Mary would fulfill. Both the reason and the season for Elizabeth had come to an end. She had successfully fulfilled her purpose. Likewise, just think what it must have been like when Jesus told His disciples that He was going away since the purpose for which He was sent was coming to an end. When He told them they could not go with Him, and they stood and watched their Messiah leave with the promise that He would come again, it must have been heartrending. The question burned within them," but when?"

The same is true of the spirit of Elizabeth, a great woman of character and purpose, pregnant with destiny. She was a powerful woman who has taught us how to carry vision and promise with dignity. We all need someone who believes in us enough to see us through to the fulfillment of our calling and election. We need someone who will propel us into destiny, showing us how to walk in faith with confidence.

God raises up mentors, spiritual mothers in Zion, who fear God and understand how the anointing flows. Some of these mentors are for a lifetime; others for a season or a reason. He places them in our lives to help us, and we can get a lot of counsel after we have made a mess.

We are triune beings; body, soul, and spirit. God created us to receive ministry in each area. Therefore, when He looked at Adam, recognizing there was no one equal to Adam in all of creation, He gave him Eve as a fitting partner. She was flesh of his flesh and bone of his bone. Consider this truth: as a man thinks in his heart, so is he. In contrast, we view ourselves based on our environment and our experiences. We ultimately attract the same people even when we know they are not good for us. When we finally "get it", and make Jesus Lord and surrender to God by his matchless power, we can change the way we think. We can reflect on how we attract people, and accept we now have the mind of Christ under the guidance of the Holy Spirit.

The Holy Spirit adjures us to be Romans 12: 1-2 Christians: *in view of God's mercy, to offer your bodies as living sacrifices, holy and pleasing to God — this is your spiritual act of worship. Do not conform any longer to the pattern of this world, but be transformed by the renewing of your mind. Then you will be able to test and approve what God's will is — his good, pleasing and perfect will. NIV*

We must have our minds renewed so we may know what is the perfect and acceptable will of God concerning us. Remember Psalm 138:8 – *God will perfect the things that concerns us.* According to II Corinthians 10:4-6, we can bring every thought into the obedience of Christ so we may have better discernment – those for or against us; those who come to use and abuse us; and those whom God has sent. Remember this – in every relationship God wants to show up.

Answering honestly more "meaning to life" questions can be a great benefit. What season am I in or experiencing right now? Am I equipped to be a friend? What is my purpose for wanting this relationship? What do I have to give? What are my expectations? Many of us have had forgettable experiences trying to be a friend. We have put trust in a friend and have failed at it miserably. We could be most eloquent on what a friend is or is not, based on our experiences. However, do we really know? Are we willing to look at what a true Godly friendship is? Let our journey begin.

We enter relationships for multiple and diverse reasons; however, the motivation for true relationship ought to be fueled by trust and transparency, mutual respect and honour, understanding, and expressed love. All true relationship can come under the microscope of the Holy Spirit and experience the refiner's fire to test its character and authenticity.

I believe we pursue relationship with different desires and opinions of individuals. We subconsciously decide the purpose, what we want out of each relationship, and then tuck this information away, somewhat like insurance against "that" day.

Reason

People are sent to us or assigned for specific purposes. Some appear to fill a need – a reason – but for only a short window of time. Others come for a season of transition from one level to a next. They last for a time until we can stand on our own. The rarest are placed in our lives for a lifetime. They leave indelible markers to which we refer often. As we cite live experiences to them, they become a plumb line, the standard by which we chart our walk.

So many times, we have an emotional need during crucial walks in the valley of decision, and receive unexpected, or even planned, visitors. During the discourse, often in simply non-committal conversations, we indirectly receive our answers to meet that need. These precious souls will come and go, so we must be sensitive so that we do not become attached in an unhealthy way. These people may have only come for the sole purpose of giving sound counsel or meeting that particular need at the time. Let me give you an example. In 1990 I encountered a visiting minister who was in town for a series of meetings for the week. Through divine connection, I had the distinct pleasure of the Godly woman's company and ministry in my home. I was very new to ministry and extremely vulnerable. We shared at such a deep level, the kind of communication reserved for long-time friends. She was like the sister every young, upcoming woman in ministry desires to have. Amazingly, God did this, offering a gift of incredible life-giving impartation. Albeit short, the time together revealed my unrealistic expectations at that juncture in my life. It was an encounter that only God could have provided with such inspiration and depth to meet my need. Today, almost 20 years later, I know, if I met her again, she probably wouldn't even remember me. She would have no idea of the impact she had on my life. She even has returned to our city, but our paths have never crossed again. She came for a reason. She took me to the throne of God, and left me there.

Season

People of different cultures who have a world vision or vice often find themselves in places, or among people, who are unbounded and different. Many times, culture shock would even cause one to wonder if we are in God's will. Let me give you an example. I remember one time our ministry was in desperate need of professional help. The Lord led a sister from a land where its customs were as different to us as night and day. We received her with gladness and depended on the Lord completely. This individual was used by God to open our understanding to the needs of our own people in Jamaica. We received the revelation that we could be missionaries in our own land. She stayed with us for two valuable years. However, in the same way she came as a "sent one", as the season with us ended, we were both aware it was time to go. Sensitivity to the Holy Spirit allowed us to release her into a new season.

Sometimes a mentor will only be present in your life for a season, so be willing to release them and move on when necessary. The Lord will bring others across your path who will help you at different stages of your journey. This can become a pitfall if we fail to comprehend the length of a season together. We must embrace the truth of seasons and apply them in our lives. In the same way there is a football season (both European and American), a basketball season, a baseball season, a cricket season, each one has a start and a finish.

Summer and winter, spring and autumn! So, too, is the same of people that we meet. Their arrival is like a breath of fresh spring air. It is so revitalizing that we wish it would never end. Like a family coming to spend the holidays, we are very accommodating – planned daily activities, extra purchases of food to fill the cupboards, and insurance of sufficient supply of everything. We even welcome the thrill of having to "bunk it", crowding into overflow spaces.

When the designated vacation time is exhausted, we can expect certain routines: packing bags and checking and re-checking for items left behind; stuffing extra luggage in an already crammed car trunk; driving to the airport in endless chatter as the minutes to departure close in. Have we told everything? Have we heard all that needs to be said? Have we gotten the latest scoops on our loved ones? Of course, have we assured the promise to come again or to visit soon? As we reach the airport, the hugs are a little tighter and longer. Have we given those final meaningful kisses that are meant to linger in our memories? Through teary eyes, we bid our loved ones goodbye. We both know it is time to go, and tomorrow will be back to routines until the expected call a week later to just check in on each other.

However, suppose the vacation of fourteen days must be prolonged for another two weeks because of unfortunate circumstances beyond control. A chemical and physiological morph comes into effect. Our overactive brain cells begin to send signals, and our attitudes change. "Oh, can I continue to feed them? What about my bills? They had better do their fair share around here! Oh no, I am not going to pick-up, wash-up, and put-up much more." Suddenly those who brought pleasure and joy are now a burden, an expense, and an inconvenience.

When did our affections change? They changed when the season ended. Oh, we still love and care for them, but we subconsciously programmed the period, and emotionally prepared ourselves, for an expected end. When these expectations become challenged, an insult occurs. We can slip into compensatory intolerance, depending on the state of our emotions and/or our current physical or environmental issues.

Human nature always prefers to be in control of its own space. In other words, we like to be in charge. To have the freedom to choose, and then decide, what is our anchor. Now, how many of us are wise enough to know that this is not necessarily how the world turns. In the changing seasons of life, let us at least attempt to access the knowledge to identify seasons as they come. Let us lean on the Holy Spirit for guidance. He always has a solution, an answer to the chaos. He will show us how to respond, especially in an overwhelming or less than favorable occurrence. He will show us the pathway to preserving relationships.

So, what do we do with an unreasonable spirit in the equation? Our dependence is unbearable. There is much need to be cautious here as the lines get crossed, and all that God intended for good, the enemy turns to evil. Satan's only purpose is to make the good, good for nothing. Idolatry, enmeshment, or co-dependency could attach itself, making our friendship or relationship unhealthy and ungodly. Where God was the center in a human being, the created becomes our counselor instead of the Creator.

We must also be aware of the "needy syndrome." This pushes us further from the desire for God toward the need for another like ourselves. We look to that person to fill needs which only God is able to do. Identifying this is crucial. Then we call to the power of God to intervene and deliver.

My third encounter was in 2005 with a mighty woman and prophet to the nations. I was introduced to her at a women's conference in Lima, Ohio where we were both invited to minister. We never really spoke, but her ministry has had such an impact on my life. I left that conference with a single tape recording of one of her teachings – Carriers or Handlers of the Anointing. I have taught this many times over to our own worship ministry team.

Hearing and meditating on this profound interpretation of the Scriptures changed my attitude toward worship forever. It propelled me into an even deeper level with a new dimension in worship. I lost contact with her, but five years later, through a dear friend, received an invitation to the "secret place" in Tampa, Florida and was reunited.

This season of my life was a roller coaster of uncertainty about my calling and living out this new way of a life of faith. However, through this one woman's ministry, I was launched into my call of destiny and purpose. I experienced God through many encounters that stripped away doubt and the fear of men. This season transported me through acceptance and value. My eyes were opened through this ministry to the amazing and inexhaustible depths of God's love.

We need one another, whether we believe it or not. People, we need each other; it is relevant to our existence. We were created this way for healthy and balanced human survival. We have friends for a reason. In life's twists and turns we need other people to assist us, unraveling the confusion, even chaos, we have woven because of ignorance, stupidity, and, more often, just sheer innocence.

Oftentimes, to fill a need for companionship in the moment, we enter, in our pure and unselfish motive, a relationship at whatever level; platonic, superficial, conversational, or just an easygoing, non-committal, simply fun release of energy. We form unholy alliances with persons of a nature contrary to what we know are healthy. Why? We have needs. Unfortunately, this need becomes the driving force, and we are unclear why we are even seeking out this particular friend in the first place. Parameters are not defined, and, ultimately, we are presented as users.

Think about it. When we need to play, we have party time friends who are full of fun and know how to have a good time. However, we are very selective with these relationships. Our friends who need "a cause" will always get on board. Remember Peter in Luke 5: 1-11 when Jesus told him to cast his net on the other side. His catch was so great he had to call for help to reap the abundant harvest of fish.

Partnering for a purpose to fulfill a specified project is another need-based relationship. These are the ones who come alongside, offering a helping hand, whatever the need, because of relationship. We form relationships to fill a variety of needs: becoming a sounding board, brainstorming as part of a think tank, being a shopping buddy, etc. Before any measure of testing, we realize we have unwittingly entered a friendship that demands more than we are willing to give. In our vernacular, this camaraderie was never intended to last long. The sociable event has become stale. We are bored, and no longer have the energy to pour into this relationship to keep it alive.

In this instance, the necessary parts of the void have been filled. Wholeness is apparent, and it is time to move on. We must take responsibility and release the situation, identifying and recalling the purpose of this engaged relationship. Call it for what it is, and move on. If we do not, we become emotionally involved in an unhealthy way. We begin to recognize the weakness and pitfalls, not only in the present relationship, but also in the individual. We can become critical and unkind. This evolves into compromise, and our circumstances become strained, even unbearable.

We are created triune beings; triune meaning as our Heavenly Father is referred – God, the Father; God, the Son; God, the Holy Ghost. God expects us to operate in all three dimensions. We are living in a body. We have a soul incorporating a mind, will, and emotions. We have a spirit through which we communicate with God. There is always an underlying reason or purpose for every relationship. Some may be selfish, yet others symbiotic in character. Genesis 1:26 says *God created us in His image and according to*

His likeness giving us dominion and saw that this was good... this was in the sixth day, the next day God rested.

Man was created in the rest of God and peace with God. God wants relationship, and that is why He created us. When man fell, God did not say, "I am finished with man," but He sought to redeem man through another; the Immaculate Conception, Emmanuel, God through the Virgin Mary, the mother of Jesus. Jesus' purpose was as mediator, a reconciler of man to God. Amazing love, what sacrifice God and Jesus made for us. I believe life is a journey, and the outcome may be out of our hands, but we still hold the key to our future. We are triune in being – body, soul, and spirit. I consider this truth: *As a man thinks in his heart, so is he.*

Who was Mary? What did she know? Why did she choose Elizabeth? These are more meaning to life questions.

Purpose

If we do not understand the purpose of a thing, we tend to abuse or misuse it. Ultimately, we destroy it, or it destroys us. What was the purpose or reason for Mary paying a visit to Elizabeth? What was God's purpose for creating man? God's purpose for creating man was because He desired relationship. More than 2000 years later, this desire has not changed.

To understand relationship and the mystery of it, we must first understand what God was after. He was after relationship, to be known by His created for who He is, not for what He can and will do. He wanted us to have revelation of who we are as His children. His ultimate desire has been to show us life in Eden, life in the garden, Kingdom life.

Relational seasons involve transition. They flow one into another. Just as the natural seasons, we can tell when they are changing. For instance, at the end of a hot summer, we begin to feel cooler breezes. The days get shorter. The colours of the trees begin to change into vibrant oranges and red. We know Autumn is here, and winter, with its frigid barrenness is not that far away, but we are assured the hope of spring will later break through. Just like these four seasons of time, our relationships find themselves moving from season to season, forming covenants.

In our relationships, we also have different levels. We have an inner circle and outer circles. We promote and demote our friends as we change our outlook on life. We maintain standards, set by us, to proceed. When you are demoted from the inner circle, it is uncomfortably clear to the one demoted. Life goes on, but we have left a trail of wounds in our wake.

We love the treasure of lifetime relationships, husband and wife, my Richard and me. It seems like already a lifetime, yet I married the man of my dreams, literally, on 7 July 1979. Honestly, I did not know men like Richard existed, and not only in our dreams. He completely swept me off my feet; what an amazing experience. After the second date, he declared he was going to marry me. Naturally, as any 19-year-old who said she was never going to get married, I found him hilarious. The rest is history now. He makes me very happy and content. I lack for nothing. He had a successful medical practice, excelling at serving his patients who loved him.

We were married for ten years, enjoying the best of the best of everything any heart would desire; travel, parties, vacations locally and internationally, trusted and loyal friends, a wonderfully wholesome and healthy atmosphere in the home to nurture our two awesome daughters; Jean-Ann Karene and Renee Antoinette who were the loves of our lives and the apple of their daddy's eyes.

Even with the freedom to come and go, enjoying our interdependence, I realized there was such a deep hole in my soul. This abyss could no longer be filled with things or friends, not even a third child. I began to cry out to God, even though I did not have a personal relationship with Him. Oh, yes, I had been a Sunday School attendee as a child, and I had prayed the "sinner's prayer", yet the emptiness was haunting.

My so affectionate father-in-law led me in prayer to Jesus as an adult. Even though I was consoled by that, I still did not know Jesus; not the way I knew was possible. I can remember one night in tears I knelt by my bed. I cried out, "I do not know You the way others do. I cannot even pray the way my children pray, but, oh, Lord, if you would intervene in my family, in my marriage, and deliver us, I promise I will serve You the rest of my life." I was thirty years old.

Our beloved third beautiful baby girl, Rochelle Marie, was the harbinger of our new season. This time was indeed the beginning of a newly transformed life -long journey. Following ten years of marriage, we transitioned from a couple cycling a worldly stand-ard of existence to a couple embracing our destiny in the service of our beloved King and Master, His Majesty, King Jesus. It was the transition in season of loving each other to loving each other in Jesus for a lifetime eternity.

Lifetime achievement awards are bestowed on many who have made a significant impact on their communities, in their com-panies where employed, or on fellow human beings. These awards suggest you have positively influenced others and have made the world a better place. Persons in our lives for a lifetime are those we consider worthy of the honor of "lifetime achieve-ment award". They have been the plumb line to our achievements and development. These are people who have shown us the world from a different viewpoint and have shaped our minds to see things from different perspectives. They are the ones who have widened our vision, opening our eyes by their actions, words, and attention. They have helped us accept ourselves as worthy of the space and time we occupy, and have catapulted us into greatness, irrespective of our vocation, profession, or trade.

Chapter 1. True Relationship
- The Journey with God

Everyone needs someone. When we are pregnant with destiny, we need someone who will believe in us; someone who will teach us how to carry the vision and promise with dignity. We need divine partnering from someone who will see us through to the fulfillment of our purpose and calling.

God raises up mentors, spiritual mothers, like those phenomenal mothers in spiritual Israel, and, also, like our Titus 2 women. (Titus 2:3-5 *Likewise, teach the older women to be reverent in the way they live, not to be slanderers or addicted to much wine, but to teach what is good. Then they can train the younger women to love their husbands and children, to be self-controlled and pure, to be busy at home, to be kind, and to be subject to their husbands, so that no one will malign the word of God. NIV) He* places them in our lives to develop confidence and competence; some for a reason, others for a season, and many for a lifetime. Moreover, they are like a sword, a two-edged sword, that cuts, heals, and delivers.

The spirit of Elizabeth identifies with the spirit and character of Christ. One of its many functions is to equip and make ready our effectiveness to eventually stand according to the vision of God's destiny and expected end. The Word of God encourages us to redeem the time. This is precisely what the spirit of Elizabeth does. In these last days, let us be fully alert to recognize and respond to the Elizabeth's who are divinely assigned to us.

An Elizabeth has answers to the myriad of unanswered questions. These answers surface from deep wells of experience. They flow through quotes and anecdotes from lips wisely guarded from on high. Knowledge gushes from a stream of unending depth and waters with workable, practical applications for growth. Our Elizabeth's are both realistic and less intimidating. They become the bridges between psychology and a spirit-filled Christian life-style.

It is amazing to see God at work in a life which, when emulated, brings true results without causing us to lose our own identities. Reputable and transparent mentors, with whom we can be comfortable, show us how to live out unquestioned potential and wield a "touch" influence. We should be discerning of our Elizabeth's as we observe the flow of anointing on them while they engage in practical day-by-day happenings. These are women with the mandate of Jesus who beckon us to come as we are; however, we will not leave the way we came. We will be changed.

Recognizing imperfections – the character flaw or the personal issue that has challenged us spiritually, physically, or emotionally – our Elizabeth takes us to Jesus and allows us to touch His outstretched hand and be made whole. With the wisdom of a skilled craftsman, Jesus shapes, hones, and chisels away, only enough to allow the masterpiece of beauty to emerge with discretion and prudence.

Knowledge is power, and the right application of that knowledge is wisdom. Proverbs 2: 5,7 says *Then you will understand the fear of the Lord and find the knowledge of God. For the Lord gives wisdom; from His mouth comes knowledge and understanding; He stores up sound wisdom for the upright.* Proverbs 2: 10-12 says *When wisdom enters the heart, and knowledge is pleasant to your soul, discretion will preserve (keep and protect) you; understanding will keep you, to deliver you from the way of evil.*

Part of our journey is in the search for our Elizabeth, the one capable of stirring up the fire inside of us. Elizabeth is a vessel of honor; a vessel in the Potter's hand. A vessel becomes a strong jar fulfilling an important role in any household. Every day it is filled with fresh water from the well, serving the family and guests; however, many moments being molded and shaped lies behind its current vital function. The potter's hands instinctively formed the mound of clay into a cone, and then to its final shape. The uniqueness of this vessel is found in the service. It quenches the thirst of all who will receive. No one is denied a drink, and the vessel is open and available to all who seek. This is Elizabeth! Her success is evident as Christ emerges in us – as Jesus said we should be His witnesses. Elizabeth teaches the practical and fragrant beauty of a life surrendered to the ministry of Christ to the world.

The strength, power, and authority of the Word is upon the tongue of the righteous. Elizabeth, operating as such, trains us to appreciate why we live in these bodies; what is the soul's purpose, and how the power of the spirit enables.

I believe that God has given all women a mandate to approve the things that are excellent in His kingdom. This excellence must be birthed through us by being rightly related, first to the "I AM" of covenant, and then to one another in covenant. We then experience excellence in ministry, in our ministerial relationships, in personal development and training, in work ethics, and in our marriage and family.

God is right now stirring a hunger in us for more. Mediocrity is not an option. Being satisfied with "just enough" is no longer a learned behavior with which we are content to live. These ungodly beliefs are pushed out, and that door is sealed tight. We look to the examples of excellence before us in the Word:

The excellent spirit of Daniel is upon us, ready now to be used by God. That excellent spirit not only helps us to discern the ungodly and what brings displeasure to our Master, but it also helps to identify God's divine providence and protection.

The spirit of Elijah, a man with sufficient faith to act as a messenger of the divine Word and to stand boldly for God in the face of impossibilities, expresses the presence of God through magnificent and special miracles.

The spirit of Deborah, so active, industrious, and caring as she moves in diligence and service, ever broadening her influence.

Oh, may our hearts hunger for us to be named among those as the Joshua's and Caleb's of our times. These were men with a different spirit; men who had faith in God that He could enable them to take the land of Canaan; men who blazed the trail for present and future generations.

Let's look specifically at approving excellence in true relationships – rightly related to God and to man. The Bible tells us that Jesus had favour with God and man. Many of us concentrate on building right relationships with our heavenly Father, and so we ought; but God also expects us to have healthy Godly relationships with our fellow brethren, nurturing the spirit of true relationships.

The actual figure of the cross is relevant - from God in heaven to us in earth and across to one another. We are joined in the middle at the heart. Anything other than this is dysfunctional, only reaping chaos, insecurity, and fear. If we do not understand the purpose of this thing (What is this thing?), we will abuse or misuse it, and ultimately it will destroy us.

God's purpose for creating man was because He desired fellowship. After more than 2000 years, His desire has not changed. In Genesis we read about God's desire to have communion or relationship. In more recent times He has desired intimacy with man. Man's fall, and consequently Adam and Eve's expulsion from the garden, has left an enormous, unimaginable void. We no longer can, like Adam, meet with God as originally intended. We have become spiritually dead to God because we sin, and God cannot fellowship with, nor even look at, sin.

To understand relationship and the mystery of it, we must first understand what God was after. The "t" in true relationship is "trust." The beautiful account of the covenant relationship between David and Jonathan, I Samuel 18: 1-4 demonstrates this.

All true relationships will be subjected to the microscope of the Holy Spirit and will experience the refiner's fire in order to test its character and authenticity.

Some of the characteristics that should be evident are belief in God, faith in God, loyalty, honesty, transparency, integrity, and confidentiality. Our desire is to display these characteristics by coming into righteousness.

When we are in a correct and healthy relation with our Father, in Jesus and the Holy Ghost, we will not have trust issues. We can be trusted, and we will be very sensitive in trusting others. This is a beautiful relationship. The carnally minded person is not committed to anything or anyone. That person will sell out to the highest bidder. Trust is up for auction and bears no allegiance to anyone. The abundance of our lives is predicted by what we believe. Once we are in right relation to God, we will choose our friends wisely. Then we can be secure in that friendship.

A trusting true friend is one who takes time to understand you. She sees you through the eyes of the spirit and is a discerner of the deeper issue, thereby giving wise counsel or sweet consolation. This trust is unsuspecting and not suspicious. She assists with your confidence without impending doom in her attitude or words. David trusted Jonathan with his life. Can I trust you with me? Can God trust you with the life of Jesus in your heart? Can He trust you to be the carrier of His anointing?

The "r" in true relationship is "respect." Convictions are what we inwardly esteem and express in our conduct, attitude, and conversation. We must show love to one another and mutual respect. Love and respect the differences in the other person. Respect the rights and opinions that are hers. We all have different gifts, talents, and preferences. We have different goals, convictions, and desires. This should not be the reason for exclusion from our company or group simply because people think differently from the way I do. There is a supply she has which could be a vital component to balance and continuity.

It is only the love and the knowledge of God that can build self-esteem and self-respect. As a man thinks in his heart, so is he. Who does God say I am? This characteristic is what we project, and other people will see and be attracted. Disrespectful behavior causes a wrong attitude.

Wrong attitude causes wrong perception, and the cycle goes on and on at a rapid rate. This cycle bears no good fruit. Disapproval triggers disrespect. People find it very difficult to follow the lead of someone they cannot respect. David had the utmost respect for Jonathan and his family, despite his father Saul's opinion of David and after the way Saul treated him. David never made Jonathan feel unwanted or threatened.

There was definitely mutual respect in their godly relationship; a relationship that was divinely inspired and orchestrated for the bigger vision and higher call. This relationship changed nations. Understanding bears the marking of godly wisdom. Godly understanding is effectively exercised in kindness and cheerfulness, without falsehood. It has with it good judgement and gives attention or consideration to even the smallest details.

A man of understanding can enter the feelings of others, can empathize and exhort with godly counsel and wisdom. Many people need people with empathy around them. The healing process really accelerates once another enters into our feelings and becomes a source of comfort and consolation.

The "u" in true relationships is for "understanding". II Corinthians 1:4 says *...who comforts us inn all our tribulation that we may be able to comfort those who are in any trouble with the comfort with which we ourselves are comforted by God.*

Understanding in its truest form can only be attained by knowing the ways of God. Psalm 103:7 says *He made known His ways to Moses, His acts to the children of Israel.* Your counsel comes only through the unction of the Holy Spirit. Our understanding of the heart hurts of one another gives us the ability to influence others unto righteousness. Understanding enhances our ability to resolve doubts and show good will with evidence that you are divinely inspired.

We know when a person's emotional state is trivialized, it triggers anger or even rage in an individual. Hurt people hurt people. Only when understanding is expressed, and one feels understood, does the darkness dispel and wounds heal. The person of understanding will be always be found on the side of righteousness and truth.

David used wisdom. He understood that Jonathan had a choice: honour his father and maintain a covenant relationship. David never made unreasonable demands on his friend, but seized every moment to stay on the side of righteousness. He protected Jonathan's honour.

The "e" in true relationship means "expressed love." I Corinthians 13 describes agape love, which is the very nature of God. The significance of agape is more than unconditional love. It is primarily a love of the will, and not emotions. God loved unbelieving humans not with emotional love, nor a love expecting something in return. He loved us with agape. God loves by His will. It is His nature to love. No matter what I say, or what I believe, or what I do, I am bankrupt without love.

Love – this is the way God has commanded us to live. From the beginning, we have heard that this is the command. A command means we do not have the option of agreeing or disagreeing. It means we do not have an opinion on the matter. We are commanded to live out of a life of love. Our lives are about love. We express, share, and care because these are the by-products of love. Love is compassion, not pity. Therefore, we can punish disobedience and still love. Pity makes us overlook disobedience and make excuses for the person. It compels us to do constant internal audits and a "love tank level check."

The love walk is never easy, but it is attainable in Christ. Learning to love unselfishly is actually a difficult task, and it demands much of "forgetting self." However, it is possible, because Jesus made that way possible.

John 15:13 says *Greater love has no one than this; to lay down one's life for his friend.* This is the epitome of expressed love, and this is our example to emulate. Love applied correctly is the healing balm to all the challenges and injuries of life. The church is likened to a hospital in its function; a place where broken lives are mended. The church is a place where the hopeless can find an anchor and the unfulfilled can find the will to both "be" and "do". It is a place where orphans can find families, and we all learn to live in harmony. Yes, the church is the place where we are taught both how special we are and how highly favored.

Even though we are assembled together in one accord as equals, the individuality of the spirit of the Lord tells us we are chosen from before the foundations of the earth. There is no one like us, for God has not created us from a template.

Affection comes through love. The physical and meaningful touch brings healing; the hugs from Jesus affection, His words of affirmation, the acts of service.

The sharing and giving of gifts and quality time speaks volume of who we are. What we have to say is important and necessary. A smile is also another way in which we express love. This love exudes from a person who embraces the expressed love of God. It cannot be faked, as it has no ulterior motives. The expression is filled with the Holy Spirit, and is, therefore, pure.

Expressed love builds confidence. It gives of self, time, finances, and privacy. It remains teachable. Expressed love makes one feel secure in the giver's company. It builds up and lifts. Expressed love fashions a team player who trusts, respects, and understands.

Jesus' purpose for coming was as a mediator to reconcile man back to God. Moreover, in doing so, He has also restored true relationship. Animal sacrifice could not satisfy, nor could it fulfill man's ultimate purpose – true relationship borne out of relationship.

Jesus is now the mediator. Written in the Scripture is God's pattern of how He ought to be worshipped. From the specific and intricate instructions given to Moses for the Tent of Meeting and his obedience to the vivid accounts of David's worship through the beautiful Psalms, we are exposed to man's expressed love for his God. We see it throughout the Scripture – the ostentatious magnificence of Solomon's temple, an acknowledgement of the might and power of God; the glory that fell on the priest as they worshipped at the temple's dedication to God; the effervescence in the writings of the Songs of Solomon; and ultimately the New Testament worship where we, who are kings and priests, can enter boldly by the blood of Jesus into true worship in spirit and in truth. A new order of priesthood has been raised up through the ultimate sacrifice of the Messiah, Jesus Christ, the Anointed One, the only Spotless Lamb.

Man is three part: body, soul, and spirit. Because of this design, man has physical, emotional, and spiritual basic needs. God has created us with an innate desire to love and to be loved, with a passion to worship. When man seeks to meet those needs, he is driven in his attempts to draw from created things, rather than from the creator, for satisfaction.

The way a man perceives himself, his world, and God will determine how he will behave and respond. Our environment and our relationship with God will determine what and who we become. It is the spirit of man that connects with God and cries out through his emotions for change, and it is through the spirit that we experience the presence of God. The first step of connection is by accepting Jesus and making Him Lord. The Word and the presence of God then develops us spiritually. John 4:23 says *Jesus said, "God is seeking true worshippers, those who worship him in spirit and in truth."*

Developing A Passion For God, The Heart Of True Worship

Psalm 84: 1-10

King David had a passion for God's presence and a zeal for His house. He spoke of how His soul pants and yearns after the courts of the Lord. His heart and his flesh hungered for the presence of the Lord so much, he envied the sparrow. Engage in praise; allow yourself to flow into spontaneous worship. True worshippers will worship; you cannot fake it.

Absorb yourself in the Word, especially the gospels. Get to know Jesus; who He is, what He said, the ministry He did while on earth. Acknowledge and learn about His authority. Becoming a worshipper in spirit and truth comes straight from the heart. This is where God looks first. A broken spirit and a contrite heart, He will not reject. God delights in the lifestyle of a worshipper. Nothing pleases him more than the quality of life displayed by a worshipper.

I remember these Words to a song by Pastor Sharon Wooten of Real Life Ministries. "Here's my worship; take joy in it; make it your dwelling place. I wanna put a smile on your face; I present my heart to You. Here's my worship...smile; here's my heart... smile; here's my life...smile.

We cooperate with the Holy Spirit and walk in the fruit. We must learn the daily discipline of submitting to the Lordship of Jesus Christ, regardless of personal emotions or circumstances of life. Let us cultivate a righteousness consciousness instead of a sin consciousness. We are warriors with a mind set on God, giving no place to the enemy. We walk and live by faith. We speak faith-filled words. We are givers without hesitation, reluctance, or resistance.

Let's be extravagant in our worship; never coming empty-handed; always having a praise. This kind of worship cannot be bought, and it will not go unnoticed. We become more obedient to the Spirit because of a deep hunger to know the ways of God.

Relationships

I believe we pursue relationships with different desires and opinions as individuals. We subconsciously decide the purpose of each relationship and tuck this information away, somewhat like insurance against "that" day. People are sent to you, or assigned to you, for a specific purpose. As I shared previously, some appear for a reason. They fill a need, but for only a short window of time. Others come for a season as we transition to the next level or until we can stand on our own. Very few are placed in our lives for a lifetime where they ultimately leave indelible markers we of refer to and live with. These people become a plumb line or standard, helping us to chart our course or walk. We have some needs in our emotions, and, when in our valley of decisions, we receive both unexpected and planned visitors. In our discourse with them, often in simply non-committal conversations, we indirectly receive our answers to meet our particular need or care. These precious souls will come and go, so we must be sensitive to the fact that we could become attached in an unhealthy way.

God will show us how to respond and conduct ourselves, especially in overwhelming situations, dealing with unreasonable spirits, and in preserving relationships without dependence. There is need to be cautious as we are apt to cross the line from what God intended for good to what the enemy tries to turn to evil. Satan's only purpose is to make the good become good for nothing.

What the enemy attempts to use to make the turn towards his destruction can be idolatry, enmeshment, or co-dependency, twisting the God-given relationship into an unhealthy, or even ungodly, one. Where God was originally the center, now the human being He created becomes our counselor instead of the Creator.

We must be aware of the "needy syndrome." This pushes us further from the desire for God and replaces that desire with a need for another like our self. We look to that person to meet the needs that only God can do. Identifying this is crucial so that we can call out to the power of God to intervene and deliver us from the faulty dependence.

Three Levels Of Relationships

When forming friendships, too often lines are crossed. It is necessary that we understand the premise of these friendships. All parties must understand what is being brought to the table and accept mutual expectations. As relationships develop, it will be necessary to revisit the purpose of the relationship and come to a mutual agreement on the next step. At all times there must be openness and clarity so that, again, lines are not crossed.

The first level is a "task" relationship. Most common examples are the employer/employee one or a contractor/contracted one. This is a job or task based on contract and expectation of payment for service within a specified period. I contract you to do a job or task, and at the end, there is an expectation for compensation. Payment for services rendered, working hours, lunch times, salaries or wages are all aspects of a task relationship.

The second level is a "supportive" relationship. Examples are father/son, mother/daughter, siblings, or best friends. You were either born into this relationship or, through God's intervention, had your hearts knit together. In I Samuel 18:1 we see the friendship of David and Jonathan on a supportive level; they were as brothers. In a supportive relationship there are no selfish motives, objectives, or agendas. It stands on its own merit. It is reciprocal with a mutual outpouring to love and to be loved. It gives and expects to receive in return – you and me and our relationship together.

There are instances where these relationships will develop in the soul, with an emotional knitting based on feelings and styles, but easily shaken when tested by fire.

The third level is a Godly covenant relationship. Covenant is a binding, solemn agreement between two parties. It has not necessarily birthed out of love, but by a work of the Holy Spirit. It is not designed by the desires of the heart but is made possible ultimately through the purposes of God to fulfill His mission on earth.

God will cause a knitting of the heart based on principles and vision. It is a supernatural love that He places in the hearts of His people. This is a connection that happens on a higher level. It combines both task and supportive levels as different stages when there is a need to affect a work together. A covenant relationship is not fed, nor does it operate, by emotions. Jesus is our example of true covenant relationship.

John 13: 34,35 says *A new commandment I give to you, that you love one another as I have loved you; that you also love one another. By this all will know that you are my disciples, if you love one another.*

Relationships should be the heart of what we are as Christians. This is exactly what God was after when He created us. The Bible is filled with accounts and examples of good, bad, ungodly, and godly relationships. Not all Christians are very good at maintaining true relationships. We serve a God of love, yet we have great difficulty communicating that love.

Often, we have not discerned the kind of relationships we are in, nor the purpose for which we have entered them. We often misunderstand the relationships, and that error results in the misuse of the essential ingredients that would have been the agents for protection. These agents act as the cement to hold together the building blocks of our relationship, insuring security, assurance, and truth.

The pressure that is placed on our friendships ultimately limits the progress and causes cracks in the foundation when boundaries are not clearly defined. We then act presumptuously because of unmet expectations, where in most instances they were unrealistic anyway. We also act presumptuously when we act on assumptions, not clarified expectations.

Betrayal In Relationship

Matthew 10: 5-17 and Matthew 5: 3-11, 13-16.

We are betrayed by those who are close to us, and usually those who we least expect. Hence, there is devastation; the great sense of loss, the gut -wrenching violation complete with sweeping, heart stopping, out-of-breath emotions that won't go away. It cries out for justice, yet it seems to evade us. Betrayal is unavoidable. Therefore, we must never take lightly the weighted and protective scripture in Proverbs 23 – *Guard our hearts above all else!*

Those who betray us usually have a piece of us that we willingly gave up to them. Amid betrayal, like offense, a lot is dependent on our heart attitude. God is always looking at our hearts. We live humbly, and humility is a learned behavior.

It was the attitude of Jesus, and must be ours as well, the attitude of the heart. Remember you can only be betrayed by someone who has your heart. Betrayal is a heart issue on both sides. That is why it hurts so much and is hard to forgive. Judas betrayed Jesus. Perhaps Judas thought Jesus could get out of that sticky situation. After all, was He not God?

Our betrayer, at times, believes we are tougher than we really are. They put our friendship on the line, not expecting the painful outcome. They are haunted by issues and hurts, memories that have not been subjected to the healing power of God. Remember hurt people hurt people.

Betrayal effects our confidence. We begin to wonder if something is wrong with us. The pain of betrayal rules many hearts; it simmers, it stifles, it sometimes shuts a person down completely. Betrayal is a destiny stealer and a vision killer. It leaves us with the scars to prove it and causes us to turn inward. It erodes our confidence for the next move of God. We construct for ourselves, cast out of our experience, a "truth" which makes us unable to hear any wise counsel.

We must apply the scriptural principles that bring comfort and hope and forgiveness. Forgiveness releases us from bitterness and the bondage of negative ties to others. Forgiveness brings deliverance, and that brings great freedom.

We must reclaim our hearts. Take our heart back and offer it again to Jesus, who is the only one who heals hurts. He understands the rejection, as He, too, had to walk that path. God is waiting and ready to touch our deepest pain, if we will let Him. He will turn our sorrow into joy. He will make us more loving in all things because of the empowering of the Holy Ghost to overcome. This is a divine exchange: we offer Him our hurts; He offers us His healing.

God takes you to another dimension as He teaches you to walk in the prevailing spirit of an overcomer. You may carry the scars, but that only proves that healing can happen through Christ. The overcomer's test of betrayal, in the moment when love is not returned, makes you independent of the fear of trusting or the bondage that comes from not believing in others. Betrayal is a part of the school of ministry. It makes you examine your own life more; pray more; and makes you better, even stronger, if you are taught by it.

Dealing With Disappointment

Disappointment means to receive unsatisfactorily less than what was expected or hoped for. Disappointment is experiencing a feeling of let down, sadness, or frustration because the outcome is less than what was anticipated. Something hoped for did not happen.

Romans 5:5 says *Now hope does not disappoint because the love of*

God has been poured out in our hearts by the Holy Spirit who was given to us." Hope does not make us ashamed because of Jesus' love penetrating the walls and sweeping through the corridors of our heart. This hope and love, which we allow to permeate our hearts, is supernatural. It does not depend on our love, which often is phileo or eros. This is liberating. It is not supported by how much we love God, or our obedience to God, but the love of God for us. There is a super abundance of this hope and love by the Holy Spirit, but it can only be appropriated by grace. Peace with God is a way to access the throne, a necessary move during affliction. There is stability in hope.

Disappointment is the enemy's work. It is a detour to our destiny. Many precious believers, prior to falling away, fell into deep disappointment about a "failed" spiritual expectation. For example, praying for a loved one whose body is writhing in pain, yet you administered the strongest medication possible. The hope of bringing comfort is distant.

We have stood on the Word, fasted, cried, given out of our need, believed and served as much time permitted, nevertheless, the loved one slips away. We are left with sad memories, and we cry, "Why God?"

Many spend their entire lives climbing the ladder of success, only to be disappointed at the end because their ladder was resting on the wrong wall. They found themselves actually going in the opposite direction. Disappointment is not just a sad emotional state of mind; it can actually sever our heart from faith. It literally disappoints us from our appointment with destiny and the will of God for our lives.

We are in the best and the blessed time. Life is filled with joy. We believe God is pleased with us, and the rewards of our labour in the kingdom are flowing. There have been many who were doing well moving toward their destiny; the future written about them seemed close enough to taste. Then Wham! A negative report. An occasion for doubt and fear. A knoll in the pathway that seems so insurmountable. We cannot get over, and we feel disappointed because of the set back.

How and why is this happening to me? Why does God not do something about it now?

By accepting this demonically manipulated attack (disappointment) into our spirits and allowing that event to germinate and grow into a disappointment with God, a bitter, cold winter overtakes our soul. Destiny remains dormant.

Where there is disappointment there is a severing from our appointment with destiny. The appointed breakthrough remains in the hand of God, but we have isolated ourselves by unbelief. We doubt that God is really for us.

Hope deferred has made our hearts sick. Proverbs 13:12. It is right there in the midst disappointment's pain that the righteous must learn to live by faith. Romans 5:5 tells us that *Hope does not disappoint.*

Satan will try to stop your purpose and destiny by putting up detour signs, but he only wins if we accept them. We have to fight and win the battle over our minds. We must become spiritual mind benders and defy the onslaught of the enemy.

Disappointments are detours whose only purpose is to kill vision Without vision, a people perish. They are destroyed. Are you carrying disappointment in your heart? Are you allowing what you see to hinder what you really believe? Have you advanced into isolating yourself?

Proverbs 18:2 says *A man who isolates himself seeks his own desire. He rages against all wise counsel.* We become immune to reason, and we spend a lot of time rehearsing the breakdown: whose fault it was, the downfall of others, even God, to produce our expected end. Proverbs 18:2 says *a fool has not delight in understanding, but in expressing his own heart.*

We must choose to renounce this thought engagement and forgive ourselves for allowing disappointment to take us off tract.

Forgive ourselves if we have failed personally or morally. Forgive, where necessary, others who have let us down.

The answer to disappointment – deepest repentance and a return to the place of worship of our Redeemer. As you worship, get lost in His presence; be found engulfed in His love; let all things, with even the scent of disappointment, fade away.

Fear not, for I am with you; be not dismayed, for I am your God. Recover yourself. Renew the intimacy with God. Enter into worship so His presence fills the atmosphere and we are overcome by his glorious company.

Your True Identity

Let the reproach that once defined you roll away. Let go of the things that hae been dead or dormant. Experience God's peace and the glory of His goodness. Do not cast away your confidence.

Hebrews 10:35,36 says *Do not, therefore, fling away your fearless confidence, for it carries a great and glorious compensation of reward. For you have need of steadfast patience and endurance so that you may perform and fully accomplish the will of God, and thus receive and carry away and enjoy to the full what is promised. Be steadfast, immovable, always abounding.*

Proverbs 24:10 says *If you faint in the day of adversity (persecution), your strength is small.*

Strength is not measured in good times, but in unfavorable ones; harsh, disappointing times and circumstances. Our confidence in God must never be cast away, for in doing so, we give the enemy legal access to our possessions. We must live in that place of persuasion and assurance of trust on the very Word of God on which we stand. This is the signal to heaven of the joyous unwavering confidence. A foundation without anxiety, an intelligent faith. The quality of confidence reinforces us to stand under pressure and spoils the enemy.

This is not carnal confidence, an open door to failure and disappointment, but Godly confidence destined for greatness.

Any lack in our life can be satisfied with God's Word. Therefore, do not cast away this confidence, for there is a reward in the now: peace, joy, and great recompense, both in this life and eternity, if we do not faint.

We must assume the attitude of expectance. Do not lose heart! Do not quit! Do not give up! God has this. He is in our corner.

Philippians 1:28 says *And do not for a moment be frightened or intimidated in anything by your opponents and adversaries, of such constancy and fearlessness will be a clear sign, proof and seal to them of their impending destruction, but a sure token and evidence of your deliverance from God.*

Our confidence in God's Word is that which brings liberty and boldness to access the throne room. Our advocate awaits and stands in defense of our cause. Our birthright, according to the scripture, is that we have been engrafted. We cry "Abba Father", with whom we have an audience. We are sons and daughters, the clear evidence that we have His favour.

Chapter 2. The Spirit of Mary

Now in the sixth month the angel Gabriel was sent by God to a city of Galilee named Nazareth, to a virgin betrothed to a man whose name was Joseph, of the house of David. The virgin's name was Mary. Having come in, the angel said to her, "Rejoice, highly favored one, the Lord is with you; blessed are you among women!" But when she saw him, she was troubled at his saying, and considered what manner of greeting this was. Then the angel said to her, "Do not be afraid, Mary, for you have found favor with God. And behold, you will conceive in your womb and bring forth a Son and shall call His name Jesus. Luke 1:26-31

We can't help but read this portion of scripture and ask ourselves, "What is truth?" Mary, who is known to all of us as the mother of Jesus, a virgin, is visited by an angel who told her she would bear the Messiah. This was no ordinary announcement and Mary knew it. She was a Jewess who completely understood the stories handed down to her through the ages. There would be a virgin birth for the Messiah. Mary stood in amazement at this incredible, impossible news. Then Mary spoke those monumental words, "be it unto me according to your word." Oh, what a visitation! In the moment, she queried, "but how can this be, since I know not a man?" Indeed, however could this be true?

In today's vernacular, picture this: a young girl, between 13-16 years old, becomes pregnant. How does she tell her mother/family? This modern-day Mary grew up in a family who strongly believes in God and practices a Christian lifestyle. What shame; what scandal is brought upon the family. We want to hide the evidence for fear of what people are going to say, so we abandon both the mother and her unborn child.

Control! We take the situation into our own hands, not mindful of tampering with a future and a destiny. We send her away to some distant relative or friend who can take care of our mess; or so we hope. Yet, a cycle of abandonment begins for the mother and her unborn child. How could God love me and allow this to happen? The ungodly belief that answers takes root in the soul. The answer has been simple to most well thinking, respected families – send her away; abortion is not an option.

Well, not much has changed in more than 2000 years of human response. Not waiting to be sent away, Mary goes to find her Elizabeth. I ask you this meaning to life question; who is your Elizabeth? Yours or mine, it doesn't really matter what our circumstance is; the circumstance is a result of simple, wrong choices. In our crisis, who can we turn to? Who will have our backs?

"BLESSED AMONG WOMEN; HIGHLY FAVOURED OF THE LORD."

Mary; who was she? She was from the lineage of King David. She was a chaste woman, a virgin, and a "ponderer" of Hebrew parentage. From a wealthy family, her father was Joachin, and her mother was Anne. Mary was pure and completely dedicated to God; a humble maiden – a devout, small town girl. Mary was well educated and knowledgeable in the Word.

God looks at the heart, and in Mary's, He found a heart after His own. Historians record Mary was 14 at the time of her betrothal. Although she was young and meek, she had a tenacity and strength of character that enlarged her capacity for the miraculous. Mary was a prime candidate for the supernatural because she was a faithful worshipper of the tribe of Judah. She worshipped in spirit and in truth, as we see demonstrated in Mary's Magnificat, the soaring song from her heart in Luke 1: 46-55.

Mary loved God and found favour with Him. She was chosen to bear the Messiah. Mary experienced a visitation when the kingdom of heaven invaded earth. What are the attributes ascribed to Mary that she could receive this high greeting: "blessed among women...highly favoured of the Lord?" How do we function in our day to day lives and remain among the "highly favoured ones?"

First, we quit using words to describe our existence as a replicated victim of circumstances, and we begin to use God's words and works to describe ourselves. Secondly, we choose to live a God-centered life. We follow the active ingredients listed for a prescription to greater breakthrough.

- Know that life is in the Word of God only.
- Seek and desire only to please God.
- No longer get entangled with the affairs of the world.
- Cultivate a lifestyle of prayer and a servant's heart.
- Remain trustworthy and worthy of confidence.
- Exert positive influence and lead by example.
- Increase our sensitivity to the promptings of the Holy Spirit.
- Study to show our ability as to rightly divide the Word of Truth.
- Live a life of giving and receiving forgiveness.

Thirdly, we speak more to what we expect, rather than setting up house at the addresses of experiences, past blunders, and unfortunate present. Lastly, we intentionally seek deliverance from being a victim to becoming a victor. Regardless of what comes our way, we declare, "God's got this."

We are in the age of discovery and definition – careers, professions, vocations. So many of us have been defined by what we have done; what we have received. We look to lifetime achievement awards but have done little to build the kingdom of God. We finish with no backbone; no flame to fuel our walk, not even a spark.

When the righteous are in authority, the people rejoice. When you leave this earth, who will know you have been here? We must take our stand. Because of secularism (without religious elements) and dualism (double mindedness), our standards have been lowered. We look to standards that are contrary to the statutes outlined in Scriptures.

We are not attracting the attention of God. We have missed the true meaning of who we are, and who God says we are. Some of us are not even satisfied with the kingdom definition. Who forms the opinion of you? Spiritual alignment is a requirement if we are to survive this wicked and perverse generation.

Mary was loved, and she was obviously a woman of character, prudence, and dignity. She had a father-daughter connection. (Unique Role of Fathers, a Manual for Father-Daughter Connection by Marilouise Rust M.A.)

Who Was Mary? What Do We Really Know About Her?

THE EARLY LIFE OF MARY – HELEN SPLARN

Documented by historians prior to 200 AD, Mary's entry into the world is no less miraculous than what happened in her teens. Her childhood equally reflects the power and presence of the divine, all prevailing God Almighty.

According to the Apocryphal (various religious writings of uncertain origin regarded by some as inspired), Mary spent her childhood, from ages 3-12, in the temple. According to historians of the twelve tribes of Israel, Joachim was a very wealthy man, but he was childless. He brought offerings twofold to the Lord, saying to himself "this is from my abundance, which will be for all the people... And this which I owe as a sin offering will be for the Lord God as a propitiation for me to appease God." Reuben, one of the twelve, stood up and said, "it is not permissible for you to bring your offering first, for you did not produce an offspring in Israel." Deeply ashamed, Jaochim left the city and went into the desert where he pitched a tent for 40 days. He said he would fast and pray until the Lord deemed him worthy.

His wife, Anne, who was barren, wept to see him go alone. She went into the garden and sat beneath the Laurel tree. Longing for a child of her own, she cried to the Lord, "Woe is me to what have I been likened to the earth? For even the earth brings forth her fruit in its season and blesses the Lord." The angel of the Lord appeared to Anne saying, "The Lord has heard your prayers, and you will conceive and give birth. Your offspring shall be spoken of in the whole inhabited world."

Anne vowed that, if she gave birth, whether the child was male or female, she would present the baby as a gift to the Lord her God. She vowed this child would be a ministering servant to the Lord all the days of its life. When Jaochim returned, Anne ran and threw herself at him saying, "Now I know that the Lord has blessed me very greatly. For behold, the widow is no longer a widow, and she who was barren has conceived."

Anne and Jaochim gave birth to a beautiful girl and called her Mary. In gratitude to God, he vowed that once the child turned 3 years old, she would be sent to the temple to be educated. Mary walked at 6 months. Her mother said God had sent her a miraculous child. She declared, "she will not walk on the earth until she is brought to the temple." Anne made a sanctuary in her bedroom and prohibited everything common and unclean from passing through it. Mary was known as the undefiled daughter of the Hebrews.

Mary was presented to Zechariah, the priest who received Mary, and prophesied over her: "The Lord has magnified your name in all generations. In you (at the end of days) the Lord will manifest his deliverance to the children of Israel."

Mary's education was astounding; she had great knowledge, insight, and understanding of the Scriptures. She lived among the holy men in the temple and was taught by them. When Mary turned 14, she was still living in the temple. Zechariah told her that it was customary for all young maidens to marry.

An angel appeared that night to Zechariah and instructed him how to choose Mary's husband. Each suitor was to bring a staff and, kneeling, pray for a sign. As they knelt to pray, all at once a lily bloomed from the widower Joseph's staff. A snow-white dove perched on the staff's tip and then flew away. Joseph – a widower, a carpenter, a builder – was astonished, crying out, "How can it be that the Lord has chosen me? I have been widowed for some time. I have sons nearly as old as this tender girl."

That day a marriage contract was signed, and the marriage celebration would be held in 12 months. This commission was a great honour. Mary returned to her parent's home, and Joseph went home to prepare a temple for his bride. "The Lord is building up Jerusalem, binding up together the outcasts of Israel. Healing broken hearts; binding up their wounds; the Lord is building. The Lord is building up Jerusalem.

Hallelujah!"

You Are Somebody. You Are Worth More Than You Think.

I Thess. 5:23,24 says Now may the God of peace Himself sanctify you completely; and may your whole spirit, soul, and body be preserved blameless at the coming of our Lord Jesus Christ. He who called you is faithful, who also will do it.

Let's look at the key words in these verses. "Sanctify" means to free from sin by a ritual of purification; made holy; the consecration of the believer; a course of life befitting those separated to God; separated from the world in behavior and conduct. "Body" is the physical form of a human. "Soul" is the sentient part of man; capable of feeling, perception, responding emotionally rather than intellectually. It is the receptive element in man that perceives, reflects, feels, and desires. It is the seat of will and purpose;

the seat of appetite. "Spirit" is the life force of a person, characterizing a living being. It is the immaterial, invisible part of man that speaks to moral qualities and activities.

"Preserved" is to keep, defend, guard, protect; to stand guard as the Roman soldier who guarded Christ. Preserved means to keep something protected from anything that would cause its current quality or condition to change, deteriorate, or fall out of use. "Blameless" is to be unblemished, guiltless, without reproach; not responsible for something wrong; doing nothing wrong or bad. Blameless does not mean sinless, it does mean free from causes for reproach and regret. Every part of our lives should bear evidence and witness that we are set apart and holy to God. The conduct of our Christian lifestyle must bear the approval of Jesus.

We live in a corner of a world etched for ourselves and with our own rules and standards. This is our safe harbor to which we retreat every now and then. In this place we have our own code of conduct based on our experiences, our environment, our training, and our exposure. This becomes the standard by which we define ourselves and judge others.

We have, even in some misguided way, written our own future and are living out self-fulfilling prophecy. I wrote a devotional entitled *I Am a Woman; Uncommon and Extraordinary Woman.* Do you know what that means? Let me share a quotation from that book.

"Woman, who is she? She has issues. She is filled with emotions. She can be extravagant and excessive. Filled with strength and endurance, dignity and grace. She was thought of with purpose and destiny. Created with sensitivity and virtue. She was fashioned skillfully and intricately, woven into a beautiful tapestry. A kaleidoscope of potential created to be fulfilled and experienced."

"Who is she? She is adaptable, frugal, and moderate. She has issues and she knows them, every one. She has dates, times, and events. She is filled with desires, unfulfilled ones. She ponders and then says, 'if I could just touch Him, just the hem.' She is filled with hope. She is determined, and she possesses power of mind."

"She is enveloped with mental toughness and physical energy. She presses in straining a force of endurance that is keeping her from giving up, not giving in, dropping out or getting short of her goal. She is an extraordinary, remarkable image of Elohim."

"The Creator, the Master Builder, He said,' Let us make one compatible, a helper; one with beauty of grace; beauty of character; with a meek and gentle spirit, beautified with salvation', and He called her WOMAN."

When did you first know in your heart that you were no longer a girl, but a woman? Was it when you had your first cycle? Was it, perhaps, at your graduation from high school or from college? When you put on your first bra? When you turned 16, or 18, maybe 21, or 30? When you had your first kiss or first became a mother? Are you still waiting to be told?

Mary recognized this when the angel visited her, announcing God's amazing message she would be the carrier of the anointing, Jesus, Emmanuel, God With Us. After that moment in time, her life was never the same.

For some of us, there is a place in our hearts where we all want to feel valued, young and free like a little girl again. Life seemed so much more fun, or was it? We still want to be cuddled and wish someone else would tell us what to do. Our stories are the same in so many ways; nevertheless, they are our stories, our experiences. That counts for a lot. These experiences are the definers of what we have become today based on the choices we have made.

However, this is not necessarily who we are. Who am I? I am woman. What does that mean? We receive all sorts of signals and messages, but very little help in becoming a woman. We live in the shadows of the infamous icon, the woman of Proverbs 31. How many times have we read this scripture and tried to find ourselves to measure up; then sadly concluding we may never measure up!

A true woman loves and celebrates herself. She savors herself as God's masterpiece, intricately designed for her time. A true woman is willing, serious, and determined to reflect the beauty and heart of Christ to her world. She seeks to live a God-centered life, trusting Him, and saying, "Yes, Lord." She knows this is only possible by His grace as she seeks to do her best in her community and to be the change agent. THERE IS FOR ME AN APPOINTED TIME!

Chapter 3. Choices and Decisions

Selfish or selfless? Life-taking, life-giving- or life-changing? We have been created with the freedom to choose. Choice is our right which distinguishes us as individuals. That fact is awesome, yet somewhat daunting. They carry such responsibility; will my choices change the world, leave it the way I found it, or pass it on in worse condition? Have you, like so many others, slipped into the indifference of "whatever's". What choices have you made lately? Please do not reply "none." It is humanly incorrect, for to do nothing is a choice. I chose Jesus! That choice was the beginning of the best thing that has ever happened to me.

Luke 4 tells us a lot about the choices Mary made. They set her on a course of events where life, as she knew it, would never be the same again. With those same choices she also set in motion the process of the redemption of mankind. What were those choices? She acknowledged the favour of the Lord to be the mother of Jesus. She chose to visit her cousin Elizabeth. Her song, the Magnificat, reflects her praise, her attitude of worship, and the acceptance of her future and destiny.

Make A Difference

To make an indelible, marked difference, we first need wisdom. Godly wisdom which begins with the fear of the Lord. James 3:17 says, *but the wisdom that is from above is first pure, then peaceable, gentle, and easy to be entreated, full of mercy and good fruits, without partiality and without hypocrisy."* So much emphasis has been placed on intellectual ascent, and, if we would just attain intellect, we would be wise. On the contrary, it is actually the spirit within that individual, the Spirit of God, which makes him intelligent. The person filled, baptized, and submitted to the power and authority of God through the Holy Spirit is the one with true understanding and knowledge. The understanding, with the right application of that knowledge, is wisdom. Mary Ruth Swope says, "True wisdom and absolute knowledge are spiritual, not soulish, in nature. Wisdom is not related to our mental ability or our level of education. Jesus is the doorway into the hidden wisdom of God."

The knowledge of who we are determines our attitude, and that, in turn, determines how well we do what we do. Some people will never come to their full potential in life because they are always looking for the easiest way out. They never stand up for anything, not even themselves.

We all have a sphere of influence, and we must seize every opportunity to make a difference. We are all leading someone who is following us. Every day, everywhere, make the most of every opportunity to tell someone about Jesus. (Dr. Richard M. Keane)

Proverbs 23:7 says *As a man thinks in his heart so is he.* " God created our bodies with five senses to be used in the decision-making process. Thoughts come through the five senses. We have the ability to decide if we want that particular thought to go past our mind to our heart. The senses help us distinguish between pleasant and unpleasant experiences; pleasure and pain." ("How We Make Our Decisions", Long Life Health, Mary Ruth Swope)

Although our taste buds function from birth, we learn as children to like certain tastes and dislike others. We touch objects that feel soft and pleasurable, while others are sharp, prickly, and uncomfortable. Our ears and nervous system find certain levels of sound soothing and others painful. Odors that we smell, or sights seen bring either happy or unhappy responses. All these responses are recorded in the brain, while it continually gathers information and stores for later use. From this collection of stored facts, we form our beliefs and make our daily decisions.

Man became a living soul when God formed him out of the dust of the ground and breathed into his nostrils the breath of life. (Genesis 2:7) The soul is composed of three parts; the mind (intellect), the emotions, and the will. The soul is housed in the body, acting as a control center. It is the seat of the decision-making powers. Our will cooperates with our mind and emotions to correlate a conclusion; "I am, or I am not;" "I will, or I will not;" "I can, or I cannot."

The soul controls our beliefs. Our beliefs are formed, modified, and solidified because of the cooperative working of our mind, will, and emotions; the threefold nature of the soul. Hence, the soul controls our behavior.

There are three key words that I believe are necessary to be at work in us to make the difference in establishing a person with good influence. These three words are not only instrumental, but critical, in the development of our character and personality; ones that would prepare us for the right to dominate our society with Godly influence. These three words are desire, decision, determination.

Desire

Mark 11:23 Whatever you desire, when you pray, believe...

Desire means to strive, long for, request, wish earnestly, and crave for the impossible.

Desire to the best YOU. Use the resources God has given you and aspire to be the best. Be discerning and flow in the fruit of the Holy Spirit – His fruit. Cultivate character; not cosmetics. Make the choice to discontinue being "vogue on the outside, but vague on the inside," and allow God to bring out all we are designed to be.

Desire will make us want to change, and it will not settle for mediocrity, but motivate us to keep working on the "best us." Desire will not allow us to continually make excuses, but to embrace the winning attitude that every day is considered an event. Achievers stay with it; they are not quitters. Desire motivates us to stay in faith and move in action. Desire is like the wind. The desire of the righteous will be granted.

I got married one month before my 20th birthday following a whirlwind romance; the kind of romance exactly like the novels I read as a young lady. I desired to be honoured, loved, and cared for just like those fictional women. I met him, my Richard, tailor made just for me, who fulfilled my desire to love and be loved.

In my earliest years of my journey with the Lord, I was pretty much on my own learning the ways of God. I never saw myself as a leader of women, let alone a pastor, until the late Denver Keane, my sister-in-law, mentor, and friend, prophesied to this end. Because I was immature and could not see what she saw, I laughed; however, I knew that deep, deep in the deepest recesses of my heart and soul, there was a tremendous desire to please the Lord. I re-live those words very often, going back to the Lord and crying out, "Can you confirm those words again?"

Growing up in an era where children were seen, and not heard, I was shy and withdrawn. In later years I was taught that shyness was not one of the fruits of the spirit. In fact, the righteous are as bold as lions.

Psalm 37: 4 says *Be delighted with the Lord. Then He will give you all your heart's desire.*

My journey with the Lord has been an adventure. I recall the desire I had to sing to Him. Recognizing worship could be my gift to Him, I just wanted to worship Him. One Sunday morning I built up the courage to minister my personal anthem, "Hunger for Holiness" by Helen Baylor. Oh, how I loved the Lord and wanted to testify to the world how much. To me, this song said it all. I got so caught up in the moment, I did not know if the song ended with the congregation's applause or silence. It was just such a blessing for the opportunity to pour out my heart.

When I took my seat, someone handed me a discreet handwritten note, "Do not ever do that again." Yes, I was crushed. However, I had to get back up! After all, what was the motive of my desire? It was to worship the Lord. I told the Lord of my desire to serve Him for the rest of my life. I felt I was to worship Him, and I did.

In another incident I was leading worship on a Sunday morning in our church. A Bible school student approached me following the service and nicely told me, "You really should go into your back yard and learn how to worship God before you attempt to lead anyone into His presence." Again, I was so embarrassed, hurt, and even offended. Returning to the Lord, again, I came to the same conclusion; "Oh Lord, I want to worship You, and this is my gift to you. I will delight myself in You."

Someone even paid for me to study with a voice coach, who told me I sounded like a train off the track and had a voice not many would wish to listen. The coach advised I could be taught technique, but to correct my voice I would have to stop singing for about six months. Now, I was really crushed. However, it didn't matter to me what I sounded like; it wasn't important to me to perform well. My desire was to surrender my gift to my Father!

All I want to do is worship... all I want to do is say His name out loud. All I want to do is lift my hands, surrender, and bow down. (Rita Springer) Did I stop singing for six months? Definitely not. Did I continue the lessons? No, I graciously stepped aside after the fees were finished. I was, however, smart enough to send my children so they could avoid the "training" I endured.

Yes, you guessed it. I still sing to the Lord in my backyard; in my bathroom; in church; when everyone is listening, and when it's just Jesus and I.

Decisions

Our environment does not determine our destiny; we must choose. (Dr. John Keane 2014) Making godly decisions will bring us favor, peace, and tender love.

The power of the un-renewed mind or carnal thoughts can be dangerous and life threatening, just as the power of believing and confession can be life changing. Romans 12: 2 says *Do not be conformed to this world but be transformed by the renewing of your mind that you may prove that which is good and acceptable and the perfect will of God.*

The mind/heart is the seat of the soul where the issues of life and past experiences can become strongholds in our lives. A stronghold is a fortress. In the spiritual sense, it is where Satan and his minions hide and remain protected. We must take responsibility for our thoughts, because the root source of our words come from our thoughts and heart.

Jeremiah 17: 9,10 says *The heart is the most deceitful thing there is, and desperately wicked.* No one can really know how bad it is. Only the Lord knows! He searches all hearts and examines deepest motives, so He can give to each person his right reward, according to his deeds – how he has lived. When you squeeze an orange, what comes out? Orange juice. When we are squeezed, what comes out?

We take authority over the gates/doors of our thoughts, bringing them into subjection, so that, under pressure, right thoughts will manifest themselves in right action. Satan offers a thought, and the next thing we know, our mouths are engaged, verbalizing that thought. Since the problem begins with the thoughts, the remedy also must begin there.

So many of the decisions have life changing consequences. They may limit the perimeters in which we exist or change life as we and our loved ones know it. Some decisions have made circumstances a lot better, making life more bearable. Others have brought to our loved ones a view beyond the now, into eternity with Jesus, life forevermore.

Many of our decisions have resulted in pain and hurt because we did not take time to look in the eyes of those we love. We chose for the moment when it seemed good for our desire. The mind is the battlefield, and it must be renewed completely for us to ever experience God's perfect plan.

The mouth will never be controlled unless and until the mind is controlled by the Word of God and the Holy Spirit. The Holy Spirit gives us clear and distinct direction, but thinking right thoughts is WORK. Our thoughts, however, direct our both our attitude and process of decision-making. The Lord has given us wisdom, insight, and discernment concerning every minuscule detail.

It has always been easier to think wrong thoughts or think the worst of any given situation. Thinking right thoughts is warfare; the mind is the territory on which Satan is most active. It is also where we experience the most defeat. According to James 1: 21 we must receive the implanted Word of God which is able to save our souls. Our souls submitted to the Word of God results in wise decisions. The Bible says to cast down wrong thoughts and negative opinions. What does that mean? Well, when wrong thoughts present themselves, we punish them. We refuse to entertain them; we refuse to give them strength.

The key to victory over wrong thoughts is to replace them with the Word. When it is hidden in our hearts and minds, it is spirit and life to us. We can cast down imaginations or high thoughts that seek to be exalted in our minds; thoughts which fight and war against the knowledge of the Word of God that is in us.

We get rid of darkness by turning on the light. We forbid wrong thoughts by closing the door on them intentionally and deliberately. We decisively turn our attention on right thoughts. We must choose. Philippians 4:8 says *Think on these things that are pure, honest, true, praiseworthy, and of good report.*

Therefore, our decision- making process must be more than will power. We must choose to become spirit led, rather than emotionally driven, so that in all our ways, God's Word is the standard by which we make choices.

Our souls must be brought under the control of our spirit. Our will power must become "won't power" as it is dictated only from the power of the Holy Ghost inside of us. Never compromise your decision for what is right. Always evaluate your present attitude and locate your heart.

The person whose desires are godly influence others, and his choices benefit all. On any given day, because it is settled in our hearts, we act to have our issues line up with God's Word and will. We want to get it right the first time around. Therefore, we get all the facts; listen carefully; ask relevant questions; and never assume nor suggest we understand when we don't. We should avoid assuming, since assumption is the lowest form of wisdom. We stay humble enough to admit when we don't understand, which earns greater respect as we do. Finally, we commit the information prayerfully, asking for wisdom to make the right choice or decision.

Our inability to decide causes instability in our lives, brings insecurity to those to whom we are accountable, and breeds mistrust and faultfinding. James 1:7 speaks about the double minded: *that person cannot suppose that he will receive anything from the Lord. He is a double-minded man, unstable in all his ways.* Promotion will overlook you, and blessing avoid you, if you cannot decide or stick to the decision you have made.

In the Bible in Daniel 8:9 Daniel made the decision not to defile himself with the food from the king's table. (to contaminate, pollute, or compromise) The decision he made, and sticking to it, gained him, not only respect and trust, but favour and influence. In the end, he was also in better health.

Daniel resolved not to defile himself with the royal food and wine, and he asked the chief official for permission to abstain. (Daniel 1:8) Daniel purposed in his heart to live a life that honoured God. That resolve resulted in Daniel's extraordinary governmental influence and in the fulfillment of his prophetic calling.

How often have we made decisions or resolutions that, in less than an hour, we then break our word, change our mind, or renege on the decision? We enter into compromise, expecting to gain favour or acceptance. Many of us begin; yet never finish. Remember it is often not how we begin, but how we finish that matters. We must decide to finish strong. Make a decision to be a person of your word, according to Psalm 15:4. Make the decision to finish what your start, according to II Timothy 4:7. Make the decision to be a person of integrity, according to Psalm 25:1 and Psalm 26: 11, 12. Make the decision to walk in truth and wisdom, according to Psalm 40:11 and Proverbs : 10-12. Make the decision to change the way we think, according to Romans 12: 1,2. Make the decision to develop good habits, according to Proverbs 3, 4: 7-9, 18-27. Finally, make the decision to associate with the right people, according to Matthew 4: 18-22.

There is the old adage, "show me your company, and I'll tell you who you are; show me your friends, and I'll know if you'll go far." We do not always get what we want, but we always live with the consequences of our choices. Coach John Wooden says, "In the end the choices you make, make you." Choices can change us for good or for evil, and, once we choose, we become a servant of that choice. It affects our life and, often, the lives of others. Decision is like the rudder of a ship; it sets our course.

Determination

Determination means to have great firmness in carrying out a purpose, a fixed direction, and commitment. Things just do not happen. We must posture ourselves in a position to finish what we have started. We must see it to the end. Determination lends itself to confidence.

The cost of determination in accomplishing a goal takes commitment and a denial that can be painful. A goal's accomplishment can be uncomfortable and unpopular when many of our contemporaries misunderstand our zeal.

Determination means there is a greater desire to achieve. Our willingness to give up something so we can achieve a goal brings us into greater things. We decide whether we will settle for success or mediocrity. By utilizing determination, we are building deeper character.

Confidence and determination come when we realize our value, self-worth, and importance. We must embrace this truth: we are valuable, and we can make a difference. We occupy a place of significance individually honed for us. We alone can occupy that place.

DESIRE is like the wind. DECISION is the rudder in the ship. DETERMINATION is the sail. Godly wisdom has already set the course. Now position the rudder; adjust the sails; and allow the wind to take you to destiny.

Chapter 4. The Spirit of Elizabeth

How would you describe your Elizabeth? As spiritual mother, mentor, confidante, spirit-filled woman, or mother in Israel? Elizabeth received a divine word as spiritual mother.

Who is a spiritual mother? A spiritual mother is always fast. That is why when trials and tribulations come, she will always last. A spiritual mother knows that God will not put more on you than you can bear. She does not use God's name in vain, neither does she swear. A spiritual mother is a part of God's divine "with me that is fine". A spiritual mother will sometimes have to rebuke.
(EXCERPTS FROM WOMEN WHO LOVED GOD BY ELIZABETH GEORGE)

WHO WAS ELIZABETH?

In the book of Luke Elizabeth is the mother of John the Baptist and the wife of Zachariah, the Temple priest. She was the older cousin of Mary, the Mother of Jesus. In the Bible, it tells of her love for reading. Elizabeth was a woman filled with wisdom of the Word who was from the priestly line of Aaron. She was faithful and trained in godliness but ordained to walk a different road; she was childless. Being barren, Elizabeth was acquainted with sorrow, shame, insults, ridicule, pain, and suffering; however, she was considered righteous before God, obedient, and blameless. These are three very important characteristics; righteous, holds the scepter on the throne; obedient, morally and ceremonially; blameless, lived a life pleasing to God, outwardly to the laws of Moses and inwardly to God.

Elizabeth kept her eyes on God. No matter how humble, simple, ordinary, or intelligent, even successful and famous, God still looks at the heart first. That is exactly what He did when He saw Elizabeth's loving heart by simple devotion. Elizabeth was chosen to bear the forerunner to Jesus, who God used to usher the kingdom of heaven coming to the earth.

Like Mary and Elizabeth, we are to be a blessing among women and to be used by God to do great things for Him in our world, wherever and whatever we define it. There is now the emergence of anointed women with a hunger for God and a passionate unction to take our place in God's plan. We want to leave our mark for other destiny seekers to follow, and to answer the call of God on our lives. Let there be no more delay!

Some women's hearts are now daring to declare "it's my time to shine", but they do not know how to bring their light forward. They are calling forth their Elizabeth, with eyes peering into every face, wondering, "Are you her?" We seek our Elizabeth with whom we will stand; receiving, teaching, training, and coaching. So many women desire to discover themselves and their functions. This can happen as they quit using their own words to describe their life and start using God's words for definition. We all need to talk what we expect; not talk what we experience.

God supernaturally causes our paths to cross via personalities, characters, different styles and makeup. They come sent! They intersect with us for a reason, a season, and even to be there for a lifetime. The Holy Spirit is given to abide with us forever. (John 15: 16). The Holy Spirit is doing exactly what He was commissioned by God to do; to equip us with the ability to discern those "arrivals." Announced or not, they are sent to inspire and propel us further on the journey set before us.

People who are passionate for God are magnetic, drawing many into their influence. We attract those of different people groups, cultures, nationals, and, interestingly, of different persuasions. However, be prepared! Even the wolves in sheep's clothing will be attracted to you, for you are a carrier of the anointing. People with passion for God have moved beyond the elementary revelation of God as provider. I have heard it said this way, "how you see God is how you will see humanity, that is how you will view your society." Passionate people see God as Moses did in Exodus 34: 6 *The Lord God is merciful and gracious, long-suffering and abounding in goodness and truth.*

True relationship begins with God, who is holy and worthy of praise and glory. The Holy Spirit is given for the purpose of abiding with us forever. Our desire must be founded on His statutes and principles, the vanguard of relationships. Without those principles, what we think is reality is only transient, superficial, and lacking substance. The fundamentals that foster true and lasting friendships is based on His statutes.

For our friendships, relationships, and acquaintances to be consequential during our time together, we must be postured as good students and disciples. At some point the student must one day become the teacher. I have been profoundly inspired by the amazing account of Elizabeth's response to Mary in Luke 2: 41: - *At the sound of your voice the baby leaped in my womb.*

Our Elizabeth's are out there – or right here. Look closer. Look at work, in homes, in the classroom. Look at executives, street vendors, entrepreneurs, business owners, classmates. Look at a friend, companion, and caregiver. Where is she? Who is she? Oh, open our eyes to see, Lord, and give us understanding to discern Your sent ones who can cast a shadow of direction in our path.

We must no longer be afraid to tap into diversity. Cross- cultural or multi-cultural women bring unlimited resources God has given us to share and to equip one another. The spirit of Elizabeth ministers to the whole woman, equipping her and helping her realize how much she has to offer her world. Elizabeth is experienced, and uses her knowledge to teach, train, and coach. Our Elizabeth propels us into being the best "me" we can be.

The woman who desires to facilitate us discovers who we are and what our function is. Then she shows us how to take our position without compromising our faith in God. She does not judge us or define us by our experience. Elizabeth is that elect woman spoken of in II John. This woman is who will teach us how to posture ourselves for the future; who will show us how to present ourselves for what is to come. This kind of woman teaches us that it is possible to stand without compromising our femininity or dignity and to retain our honour graciously.

Women of faith can show us their Christianity without ever hiding their humanity. We want to be groomed by the woman spoken of in Titus 2:3-4 AMP. *Bid the older women similarly to be reverent and devout in their deportment as becomes those engaged in sacred service, not slanderers or slaves to drink. They are to give good counsel and be teachers of what is right and noble, so that they will wisely train the young women to be sane and sober of mind (temperate, disciplined) and to love their husbands and their children...*

May I suggest that the older woman referred to has more to do with wisdom that revelation gives than age or chronological reference. This woman is experienced.

As we desire to be the best "me" we can be, we ultimately fulfill the great commission. We want our Elizabeth's ministry to be toward the whole woman and with an objective of equipping us. God's gifted creation (emphasis on the truth we are each gifted) has come this far and now has something to offer another sister. The student, then, one day becomes the teacher.

Our Elizabeth has limitless possibilities; she could be a person or a place, a place of grace and peace in atmosphere and spirit at the mercy seat of God. Our Elizabeth represents our "healing company;" the healing company that is a networking of bodies positioned for "finishing" and teaching us how necessary waiting until our time comes is. Therefore, when she turns like a diamond, she shines and sparkles, not from trendy attire, immaculately adorned pearly hair, or exquisite jewelry, but because of the holy oil of the anointing.

She is the woman in your life who says, "Now is your time to shine. You have been groomed and it is your time to bloom." She is that mother, sister, friend who helps you discover who you are and how to function in this exciting, amazing thing called life.

The Spirit of Elizabeth exercises great patience, showing us how to assume our place without judging. She is trained and knowledgeable in posture facilitation, never compromising our femininity, faith in God, and Christian stand.

The King is here. The path of the just shines unto an even brighter day. Our healing company tells us we are somebody, and worth far more than we think. Every Mary needs an Elizabeth. Who is our ultimate Elizabeth? Elizabeth is Jesus; the one who sticks closer than a natural brother; the one who is a man for all seasons; the one who is always relevant in my reasoning and current in my season. The spirit of Elizabeth, Jesus, is present for a lifetime and beyond.... For all eternity.

Chapter 5. Godly Confidence through Detours of Destiny

DO NOT CAST AWAY YOUR CONFIDENCE
APPROVE THE THINGS THAT ARE EXCELLENT

Do you need acceptance? Are you feeling unwanted, abandoned, and rejected? Do not cast away your confidence! It is your access and your liberty to God. It is the right approach to His throne. Come boldly!

The following scriptures remind us of God's promise to us. Hebrews 10: 35 says, *do not therefore fling away your fearless confidence, for it carries a great and glorious compensation of reward.*

Hebrews 10:36 continues, *for you have need of steadfast patience and endurance so that you may perform and fully accomplish the will of God, and thus receive and carry away and enjoy to the full what is promised, be steadfast, immovable, always abounding."*

Proverbs 24: 10 tells us, *if you faint in the day of adversity (persecution) your strength is small. Strength is not measured in good times, but in unfavorable, harsh, disappointing time and circumstance.*

We must never cast away our confidence in God. If we do, we give the enemy legal access to our possessions. We must live in that place of persuasion, in an assurance of trust, in the very Word of God on which we stand. This is the signal to heaven of our joyous unwavering confidence; a foundation without anxiety and an intelligent faith. Quality of confidence reinforces us to stand under pressure and thwarts the enemy.

This is not a carnal confidence that can open doors to failure and disappointment. It is a godly confidence destined for greatness. Any lack in our lives can be satisfied with God's Word; therefore, do not cast away this confidence. There is a reward in the now. If we do not faint, there is peace, joy, and great recompense in this life and in eternity.

We must assume the attitude of expectancy, and do not lose heart! Do not quit! Do not give up! God's got this, and He is in our corner. Philippians 1: 28 says, *and do not for a moment be frightened or intimidated in anything by your opponents and adversaries, of such constancy and fearlessness will be a clear sign, proof and seal to them of their impending destruction, but a sure token and evidence of your deliverance that is from God.*

Our confidence in God's Word brings liberty and boldness to access the Throne Room where our advocate stands in defense of our cause. Our birthright, according to the Scriptures, tells us that we are engrafted, and we cry, "Abba Father." We have an audience. We are sons and daughters; the clear evidence that we have His favour.

Often, we lose confidence when we meet opposition and intimidation. We lose confidence to anger, self-doubt, fear, criticism, sickness, disappointments, persecution and rejection. The Bible says when we are persecuted for righteousness sake, we should rejoice. We lose confidence in the testing of relationship and friendships. Listen, we may not always agree on some issues, but let us find the ones we can, and then grow into maturing friends. I believe that friendships are forever through the contributions made to this wonderful, or not so charming, present persona. It ultimately is up to us to make the most from every relationship.

God has given us so many rich and precious promises in His Word. We are more than conquerors. Why should we then throw away our confidence in life-giving promises like these: eternal life through Jesus Christ (John 10: 28), sufficient grace (II Cor. 12: 9), and His everlasting presence and love (Joshua 1: 9). Oh, beloved, what then shall we say to these things? If God be for us, who can be against us?

I have told you these things so that in me you may have perfect peace and confidence. In the world you have tribulation, trials, distress, and frustration, but be of good cheer. Take courage; be certain and undaunted! For I have overcome the world. I have deprived it of power to harm you and have conquered it for you. John 16: 33

Detours In The Midst Of Destiny

Joseph, a true statesman of Egypt, began his challenges of fulfilling the call with his early coat of many colors. (See Genesis 37: 3 *Now Israel loved Joseph more than all his children, because he was the son of his old age. Also, he made him a tunic of many colors*)

This year will be a new beginning of dreams finding fulfillment. With every dream, every vision, and every promised land, there is a challenge and opportunity to overcome. The coat of many colors that was given to Joseph by his father is a picture of what God gives us to put on.

God is a God of color, of diversity, of beauty, and of brightness. He takes us beyond the place of dull grey, calling us to dream beyond ourselves to a place of overflow that affects others. Joseph, who first had to overcome many things, saw the God-given dreams come to pass when, in a moment, he inherited a kingdom. We, too, when the fullness of time arrives for our dreams, will see our faithful God bring them to pass.

Our faithfulness, commitment, and uncompromising heart are required to inherit the fullness of what God has for each of us. In order to inherit a promise, we must have a dream with the accompanying grace to overcome in the seasons of life that are packaged with these dreams. (Quote by John Belt 14/08/13)

As an example, read the book of Acts. From the Damascus Road experience of Saul's transformation to Paul in Acts 9 to the end of the entire book is a recount of Paul's detours he took on his way to the fulfillment of his call. Acts 20: 24 says, *but none of these things move me, nor do I hold my life dear to myself, so that I may finish my race with joy.* Paul could declare with authority in Galatians 6:17 *from now on let no one trouble me for I bear in my body the mark of the Lord Jesus.*

How Did You Get Here?

We need our GPS (God's Protection and Sovereignty) tuned into the frequency of heaven so we do not lose faith or become weary.

A detour is a roundabout or circuitous way of course. It is an indirect procedure or path. Sometimes detours are necessary. God enters so He can take over; to get control of our lives and steer us in the right direction. On the way to our destiny, He takes us through a process of character building.

Destiny is the predetermined, usually inevitable, irresistible course of events. As devastating as these detours may seem, especially when they make no sense and when every attempt to understand fails miserably most of the time, they have a purpose in our lives.

All of us, if we have been around Christians or church circles long enough, have received a word, scripture, or have heard a sermon or encouragement, that pointed us toward our destiny or purpose. Joseph had a dream and was hated for it (Genesis 37); Mary was visited by an angel (Luke 1:26-38); Jacob's mother took matters into her own hands, even though the Lord gave her instructions regarding her two sons (Genesis 25: 23).

You have a word! In the middle of rejoicing, DETOUR! Detours appear in different shapes and forms; for example, people can trigger an unexpected detour through betrayal, loss of a loved one, divorce, distasteful relationships, or character assassination. Disaster can result from indiscretions. Devastation comes in the aftermath of life's storms.

All these examples carry with them disappointment. When we are dis-appointed, we are cut off from our appointment with destiny. Our appointed breakthrough remains in the heart of God, but we become isolated by unbelief. Hope deferred has made our heart sick; yet, it is here, in the throes of disappointment, that the righteous learn to live by faith. (Hab. 2: 104) Emotional traumas, abortions, unwanted pregnancy, relocation, financial collapse, etc. are all potential re-routing events, but do not despise the detours of life. Let us choose to honour the journey.

God Has A Plan And We Are All Part Of It

Think of Jacob, who took a major detour and ended up with two wives. (Genesis 29: 15-29) What about Joseph? He also had a major detour; sold into slavery and imprisoned, all because God gave him a dream. Consider Mary, the mother of Jesus. She encountered a colossal detour – betrothed to be married and gets pregnant. Where is the Daddy? Joseph is told to marry her anyway and father the child. However, they heard from the Lord!

We, also, may have heard from the Lord. When we do, we have had our Kairos moment in His presence, and He has saturated us. But suddenly there are DETOURS! The doors to our destiny seem to close. We are tempted to turn back and doubt God! Do not fear; do not cast away our confidence. Honour the journey. Many times, the detours amid our destiny are there to teach us. God wants to get our attention. Jesus said that we are crossing over; we are going to the other side. (Matthew 8:18)

What do we do when this happens? We go back to the anointing.

Take us back, Dear Lord, to the place when we first believed. We need the anointing; saturating us, empowering us to not give up; pressing us on to our breakthrough.

Don't give up. I know the devil's been in and out, back and forth, in your life. He's been in your thoughts, jumping up and down in your business. He's been messing with your destiny and purpose; nevertheless, don't let fear take you off track, off course with no detour signs. Yes, you are about to give up. You feel like you just cannot take it anymore.

You are right on the brink of a breakthrough! Can you see it? Oh, God's grace is keeping you. His mercy is enduring in every situation. You are alive today only because of His grace. You may have been distressed, defeated, complacent, and harbored moments of compromise. You may have been depressed, broke, and broken. Don't give up but know your purpose. It will define you and determine how life goes hereafter.

Get Back Up On Your Feet

Keep on your armor. Have the determination and tenacity to keep your faith alive and active. Keep on loving; keep on giving; keep on living for Christ. Keep on believing the best and guard your heart against offense.

Remember we all have an inheritance that has been promised. God will complete whatever is lacking as we are obedient. Refuse to become discouraged, and do not even consider it as an option. Proverbs 24: 10 tells us *for if you faint in the day of adversity, your strength is small.*

Your destiny is sure. It has already been written, and it has been guaranteed. Change your address and move on in an attitude of expectancy.

Dealing With Betrayal In Relationship

ONE DETOUR TO YOUR DESTINY

Matthew 10: 5-17, Matthew 5: 3-11, 13-16

Have you ever felt betrayed by a friend or by someone you dearly loved? When it happened, did you feel like that person put a knife in your back by violating your trust? Maybe she revealed things that should have been kept in confidence. Did you wonder how a person so dear could be used by the devil to attack you in such a vicious way?

Betrayal is something that has happened to people since the beginning of time. It is simply a fact that the devil is a master at distorting and ruining relationships. He knows how to lure people into situations where they end up feeling offended or hurt. Then he coaxes the person to nurture the offense until it mutates into strife that separates even the best of friends and family. (Excerpt from Sparkling Gems, Rick Renner)

We are betrayed by those close to us, usually by the ones we least expect; hence, the resultant devastation. The hardest part to handle is the great sense of loss. As the gut-wrenching violation sweeps over us, our heart seems to stop, and breath is hard to draw. The emotion won't seem to go away, and we cry out for justice that continues to evade us.

Betrayal is unavoidable; therefore, we must never take lightly the weighted and protective scripture in Proverbs 23: *Guard your hearts above all else.* Those who betray us somehow retain a piece of us which we willingly gave up to them.

In the midst of betrayal, like offense, a lot is dependent on our heart attitude. God is always looking at our hearts. The attitude of the heart must be humble. Humility, a learned behavior, was the attitude of Jesus and must be ours as well.

Remember, you can only be betrayed by someone who has your heart. That is why it hurts so much. Betrayal is a heart issue on both sides, and, because we hurt so much, find it hard to forgive. Judas betrayed Jesus. He believed Jesus could have gotten out of that sticky situation; after all, was He not God?

Our betrayer, at times, believes we are tougher than we are. They can put our friendship on the line. Not expecting the painful outcome, they are haunted by issues and hurts. They have memories which were not surrendered to God's healing power; hence, hurt people hurt people.

Betrayal affects our confidence. We begin to wonder if something is wrong with us. The pain of betrayal rules many hearts; it simmers, stifles, and sometimes shuts a person down completely. It is a destiny stealer and a vision killer, leaving us with the scars to prove it. It causes us to turn inward. It then erodes our confidence for the next move of God since we have consequentially constructed "a truth", cast out of our experience, that makes us unable to hear any wise counsel.

We must apply scriptural principles in the fear of the Lord to forgiveness, which brings comfort and hope. Forgiveness releases us from bitterness and delivers us from the bondage of negative ties to others. What great freedom forgiveness brings. We must reclaim our heart; take it back and offer it again to Jesus, the only one who heals hurts. He understands the rejection. He, too, had to walk that path. God is waiting and ready to touch our deepest pain, if we will let Him. He will turn our sorrow into joy. Because of the empowerment of the Holy Ghost to overcome, we can become more loving in all things.

How then should we conduct ourselves in the fear of the Lord? It happens in a divine exchange – we offer Him our hurts, and He offers us His healing. God takes you to another dimension as He teaches you to walk in the prevailing spirit of an overcomer. Be advised that, although we are overcomers, we still bear scars. Wear the scars proudly as proof all things can be done through

Christ.

There is a test of betrayal. The exam is passed when, in the moment when love is not returned, you become independent of that fear of trust, you are delivered from bondage of not believing in others. Betrayal is a part of your school of ministry. It makes you examine your own life more and pray more. Betrayal actually makes you better and stronger, if you are taught by it.

I Peter 1: 13-21 says *Be sober minded in opinion, as well as in practice.* Be humble in your judgement and have a strong, perfect trust in the God's grace. Let holiness be your desire and duty; have holy confidence in God as a father and an overwhelming fear of Him as a judge. When we regard Him as judge, it also makes Him dear to us as our Father.

(See Word for Today, May 25, 2016 "What Causes Discouragement")

Disappointment And Discouragement

OTHER DETOURS TO DESTINY

Disappointment means to receive less than what was expected or hoped for satisfaction. Disappointment is experiencing a feeling of being let down; sadness or even frustration because the outcome is less than what was anticipated. Something hoped for did not happen.

Romans 5: 5 says *Now, hope does not disappoint because the love of God has been poured out in our hearts by the Holy Spirit who was given to us.* Hope does not make us ashamed since Jesus' love penetrates the walls and sweeps through the corridors of our heart. This hope and love that we allow to permeate our hearts is supernatural. It does not depend on our love, which often is philia or Eros. This is liberating! It is not supported by how much we love God, or our obedience to God, but by the love of God for us.

There is a superabundance of this hope and love by the Holy Spirit, but it can only be appropriated by grace. Peace with God is a way to access the throne, which is useful in affliction and for the stability in hope. Disappointment is one of the many tactics of the enemy's work to detour us away from our destiny. Many precious believers, prior to falling away, fell into deep disappointment over a "failed" spiritual expectation. As an example, we may have been praying for a loved one whose body is writhing in pain. Having administered the strongest medications, options are now exhausted. The hope of bringing comfort is distant. We have stood on the Word, fasted, cried, given out of our need, believed, and served as much as time would permit; nevertheless, our beloved has slipped away, and we are left only with sad memories. We cry out, Why God?

Many spend their entire life climbing their ladder of success, only to be disappointed at the end because their ladder was resting on the wrong wall. It may even have been going in the opposite direction. Disappointment is not just a sad emotional state of mind. It can actually sever our heart from faith. It literally dis-appoints us from our appointment with destiny and the will of God for our lives. What happens when we are in the will of God for our lives, fulfilling destiny? We are in the best and the blessed of times. Life is filled with joy. We believe God is pleased with us, and the rewards for our labour in the kingdom are being rewarded.

There have been many who were doing well, moving toward their destiny. God's future written about them seemed close enough to taste. Then WHAM! A negative report, an occasion for doubt and fear. The knoll in our path seems so insurmountable, we believe we can never get over. We feel disappointed at the set back. How and why is this happening to me? Why doesn't God do something about it now?

By accepting this demonically manipulated attack (disappointment) into our spirit and allowing it to germinate and grow into a disappointment with God, a bitter cold winter overtakes our soul, and destiny is dormant. Where there is disappointment, our appointment with destiny is severed. The appointed breakthrough remains in the hand of God, but we have isolated ourselves through doubt and unbelief that God is really for us.

Hope deferred has made our heart sick. (Proverbs 13: 12) However, right there, amid disappointment's pain, the righteous man learns to live by faith. Romans 5: 5 tells us that hope does not disappoint. Satan will try to stop purpose and destiny by putting up detour signs, but he only wins when you accept them. We must fight and win the battle over our minds. We must become spiritual mind benders and defy the onslaught of the enemy. Disappointments are detours whose only purpose is to kill vision. Without vision, a people perish and are destroyed.

Are you carrying disappointment in your heart? Are you allowing what you see to hinder what you really believe? Have you advanced into isolating yourself? Proverbs 18: 1 says *A man who isolates himself seeks his own desire; he rages against all wise counsel.* We become immune to reason, and we spend a lot of time rehearsing the breakdown. Whose fault was it, the downfall of others or even God, that our expected end vanished. The Bible says a fool has no delight in understanding, but in expressing his own heart. (Proverbs 18:2) We must choose to renounce this thought and return to engagement. We need to forgive ourselves for allowing disappointment to take us off track.

We need to forgive ourselves if we have failed, personally or morally. We also need to forgive others, where necessary, when they have let us down. Disappointment quickly fades away when we do the following: deeply repent, return to the place of our Redeemer's worship, get lost in His presence and found in His love, and let all things with even a scent of disappointment go. Fear not, for I am with you...Be not dismayed, for I am your God. Recover yourself; protect yourself; keep your heart in Eden. Consider these actions to keep your heart in a good position: protect, attend, be circumspect, take heed, look narrowly, observe, preserve, regard, save, watch, and discern.

We need to renew our intimacy with God in worship so that His presence will fill the atmosphere, and we can be overcome as He fills us with His glory. Your real identity is to let Him be seen in you. Let the reproach that once defined you roll away. Let go of the things that have been dead or dormant.

Experience God's peace and the glory of His goodness. Let us locate our hearts. Let us go to Eden where the atmosphere is charged with the presence of possibilities, where healing streams flow from The Source, where new beginnings happen. Eden is the place God created to fellowship with man. (Genesis 2: 15) Eden is where it all began. God, putting man in His heart, gave man His heart to keep and tend. Because of this, we can know God and can love Him as He is. This revelation is incredible, untimely, and indescribable! This is the Glory! The place of His presence; the atmosphere of His glory. Access has been restored to us by the blood of Jesus.

Eden is described as the garden of delight; a place where desires are fulfilled, a place of God's blessings and prosperity. A heart that is prospering is a heart that is not limited to emotions only. Keeping our hearts in Eden include experiences of beauty. We see through the eyes of agape; the things that are true, pure, praiseworthy, honest, and virtuous.

The atmosphere of Eden promotes fruit bearing. It is a well - watered pleasure ground; a paradise where the heart, mind, and tongue are connected. Therefore, if God can get us to keep our hearts in Eden, then certainly our tongues will be kept submitted and in check. *Guard your hearts with all diligence, for out of it flows the issues of life.* (Proverbs 4: 23) We already know we are the product of our thoughts; we also determine our destinies by our speech. We have given life to so many adversities and have plagued many simply by what we confessed.

Eden is the place where we find living water, and, as we drink, find we never thirst again. We find abundant grace there to both live and give life. God will find us true to our worship there; one spirit, one heart.

The heart is the seat of our affections, intellect, and our will. The heart and head, or mind, act and react to one another. The heart is replete with ambition, passion, and appetite. It is the controller of the will and action; the innermost centre of the natural condition of man. It is the reservoir of the entire life power. Heart issues are important to God. His desire is for our hearts to be at peace, so we can fellowship with Him and enjoy Him. From the abundance of the heart the mouth speaks life or death; sweet and bitter water cannot come from the same fountain.

To strengthen our heart is to be empowered by the Word. Why? The Word is living, powerful and active. It is sharp and judges the motives of our heart. The Word locates us. Strengthening the act becomes the strengthening of the whole man because the heart is the center of the rational and spiritual nature of man.

When a man presumes in his heart, there is a false sense of confidence. The man who stands firm upon the Word in his heart becomes strong-minded with purpose. He is not forced but has control over his own will. The heart submitted to the Word of God grows more and more into the image of God and is beautiful in elevation before the Lord. The submitted heart becomes an "ask what you will, and my Father will give it" heart.

Men look at the outward appearance, but God looks at the heart. It is where He wants to inhabit and express His love to others. God looks through our heart, because the heart is the seat of love and hate. It is the center of thoughts and concepts. The heart is compliant to God's influence. With the heart we know, understand, and reflect; from it exudes joy and acceptance and emits rejection and pain. The heart is the receptacle of God's love; the indwelling place of Christ. It is the field for the seed of the divine Word. It is the place where the shalom of God abides and finds the closet of secret communion with God.

A root of rejection is a sure detour around fulfilling our destiny. Closing this door is primal to getting us back on track through healing. Dealing with rejection is a matter of the heart. Keeping our hearts in Eden is the answer to living out this love walk here on earth.

Chapter 6. The God Journey of True Relationship

Relationships should be the heart of what we are as Christians since this is exactly what God was after when He created us. The Bible is filled with accounts and examples of good and bad, godly and ungodly relationships. Not all Christians are very good at maintaining true relationships. We serve a God of love, yet we have great difficulty communicating that love. Often, we have not discerned the kind of relationship we are in, nor the purpose for which we have entered it. There are agents that cement, protect, and hold together the building blocks of our relationship, making it sure and true, but we misuse these essential ingredients.

The pressure that is placed on our friendships ultimately limits the progress and causes cracks in the foundation. This happens when boundaries are not clearly defined, and we act presumptuously. Unrealistic expectations that then result in unmet expectations, or actions based on assumption, can lead to stress fractures.

I had the greatest opportunity to experience all three levels of relationship in one. It began almost like a task. I met Margaret more than 32 years ago, and she became my very close and best friend. I went to an interview for a customer service agent position at the prestigious Air Jamaica, the pride of our nation at that time. It was an interesting, yet pretty awkward, meeting. After the second encounter in the rest room, she invited me to have lunch.

We were as different in temperament and personality as oil is with water. My born-again experience was yet a thing of the future. Margaret was loved by everyone; she had a warm, sweet, inviting persona. She carried with her that spirit that invited you to tell her anything, and it was safe. Margaret had the ability to appreciate you for what and where you were. She was "miss cool"; I, on the other hand, did not make friends very early or easily, so I did not have many. I had deep trust issues due to an internal crater of rejection I carried with me everywhere.

We worked closely together for about two years. Then I left the airline and joined Air Canada part-time. Our friendship continued despite the changes, and Margaret remained supportive. I could call on her anytime for anything. She was the kind of person that could make things happen in the most challenging situations. She always seemed "to know a guy" who had far reaching influence; however, she became my only friend.

We began traveling a lot together, even as far as London, England to visit my Uncle Frank, and we had such fun. Our children, all girls who were approximately the same age, also became long-standing friends, as well as our husbands. There were many joint family times, sleepovers, and barbeques. Our families literally fused together, which was amazing even outside of Christ. Over the years we became inseparable. Even when I left secular employment to pursue a business on my own, Margaret remained my dearest, most trusted friend. She would take her days off from her job, and jump on board to assist my business, no strings attached.

When my family and I had our re-born experience, her husband and children followed suit, but not Margaret. I maintained our friendship, trying to be a good witness, and hoping she would also be attracted to Jesus. However, it soon became a struggle; uncomfortable for both of us in our separate beliefs and different values. I loved my friend, but I loved Jesus more.

Eventually, the boldness of the Holy Spirit came upon me, and I opened up with my feelings. Our friendship could not continue, for I knew I would enter into compromise. This was a very hard thing to do, and I hurt my friend very much. We had a soul bond, and it was so difficult to release my only true friend. I was so very lonely. Our family prayed, and I know her husband and girls were praying, too.

This family, although they lived about an hour away, showed up every Sunday and for all mid-week meetings. Margaret's husband became my husband's right hand as we took on leadership of the church. Eventually, my husband gave up his medical practice, and I gave up my business. Together we went into full-time ministry. God is faithful to keep watch over His saints and to answer our prayers. Margaret finally began coming to church; she even later resigned her job and became the church's accountant. By now, we had passed the test of "task relationship" and "supportive relationship" and entered covenant relationship. We remained such until she went home to be with the Lord in June 2013. Margaret was a true and faithful friend; we loved each other.

The Blessing Of Good-Bye

My niece, Julie-Ann, sent me the following from her own writing. *I believe this sums up the journey of true relationships. There are relationships, friendships, associates, and affiliates in your life for which the doors have been closed. Never try to reopen and re-establish connections. Many times, it is God's way of ending those seasons.*

Your life's journey does not consist of the same people all the way from start to destiny. Let them fall by the wayside and move on with those God has chosen to hold your hand in your next season.

You see, the terrain might change, depending on the route God leads you. The people who walked one leg of the journey may not be fit to tackle the sudden change to higher ground. They might stand at the bottom, pause, look at you, and think, "Where is she going?" "Why are you going that way?" "You must be crazy; this could never be right." They simply cannot come with you, friend. Walk on through the wind, the rain, and the rough terrain of hills and valleys. If God has plotted a path for you, He will provide you with the ability to walk the path ahead without the associations you left behind. Their duty or assignment to walk you through a part of the journey has ended.

As you walk, you will see new associations along the way, strategically placed to support and accompany you along this new part of your journey and destiny. God has positioned them to understand the terrain and to have already developed strategy to handle it. Never feel bad about leaving the others behind. It is all part of the divine plan. Be prepared many will not understand the journey and may even mock you, speak negative things to you, or cause you to slow down, pause, doubt, or even turn back. They simply cannot understand, nor can they appreciate your journey.

Life is filled with seasons; old and new. Doors open and close. Begin to embrace your seasons, the sudden changes in your terrain with corresponding elimination processes along the way. Remember not everyone is called to walk with you from beginning to end. Learn to let go, move ahead, and embrace the new walking partners God has provided for you. The gift of good-bye is a great gift, a sure blessing. It saves your purpose and protects your destiny. Never question it or feel bad about it all. It can save you from falling, slipping, and stopping due to the negative noise on your way through life. I repeat, not everyone will walk with you all the way. Kiss them good-bye and walk on into your God given destiny.

Chapter 7. Entrusted Anointing

Can God Trust You With His Anointing

The anointing does not belong to us; neither can it be owned nor manipulated. The anointing, in my opinion, is the power gift of God's presence for establishing kingdom order and authority. God created man and woman in His likeness and image. He created us equal, but not the same; the same nature, but not interchangeable. There is no need for striving for equality because God has made us equal. Adam sold out to Satan, but God redeemed us at Calvary. It is a done deal. Redemption is complete, and, therefore, we are complete in Him who is head over all principalities and powers. (Colossians 2: 9,10) But do we believe like Mary did in Luke 1: 45: Blessed is she who believed there will be a fulfillment of those things which were told her from the Lord?

What influences you? Whatever is influencing your heart will determine the standard that is raised and how much God can do to fulfill His Word. We must know what we believe and why. We must know what we base that belief on and why, so our beliefs aren't necessarily according to what someone else says. We must be likened to the Berean Christians referred to in the book of Acts who searched the Scriptures. We must desire the spirit of the sons of Issachar who could discern the times and direct the nation of Israel. The Holy Spirit is saying the same thing to different people in different ways. What is he saying to you? Those who have ears let them hear what the spirit of the Lord is saying. Remember God is always speaking - we are the ones with the hearing problem.

What promise has God made to you, and have you believed? God is seeking true worshippers. (John 4: 23). He is also seeking women He can trust with His Word. His eyes go to and fro in this earth, searching for hearts that are loyal to Him. (II Cor.) We are mandated to become faithful witnesses to every generation. We must first become faithful in the little things for us to be blessed with much. This can be done by simply sitting at Jesus' feet, it is through this intimacy with Him that you will begin understand the different seasons and times as He works in your life. You will begin to see your life become fruitful as God has placed a deposit in you and He will cause it to manifest.

This yoke destroying, burden removing power of God's anointing does not belong to us, we have to prepare ourselves to receive of this wonderful gift. We must learn what obedience and true submission is and put God in charge. This anointing will cause us to be stripped, purified and sanctified so that God's character can be molded in us. It requires the sifting of the chaff, working out the issues and works of the flesh - putting them aside; it comes with the expulsion of all that is detestable to God and in the end it is worth it.

Know that you have to be patient with yourself as God is not in a hurry and do not let go until He blesses you!

Chapter 8. God's Got This

SEEING THROUGH THE EYES OF LOVE

KEEPING YOUR HEART IN EDEN
Proverbs 4:18 says But the good man walks along in the ever-brightening light of God's favour; the dawn gives way to morning splendor. The path of the just shines even unto a brighter day.

Every morning sitting across from each other in our bedroom, Richard and I would read the Word of God, pray, and share what we believe the Holy Spirit had spoken to us. It could be through our own personal devotions, as we received a spiritual download of revelation during the night, or as we prayed.

Our prayers would often be for others who had been over-taken by unfortunate "suddenlies", interceding as the Spirit would lead. Many prayers were in thanksgiving to the Lord for keeping us both in health and for giving us life to see another day. We offered prayers of commitment to serve Him even more in that day.

It was November 2014, our 25th anniversary of ministry, and the Word through Bishop Dr. Levy Knox was "after these things, it is up from here," based on
Habakkuk's *After this day, I will bless you.* We enthusiastically echoed these words and declared them over the church. What joy; what enthusiasm; what conviction. We all believed this was

it; we were embarking on a great move of God in the faith realm. We were at the height of celebration.

We had received two previous words in anniversary services. Following the theme of I Samuel 30 when King David, who had been violated by the enemy, received instruction from God: pursue, overtake, and without fail, recover all. The word prior to that was Family Church on the Rock was in "the crossover." We studied that out - when the Israelites crossed the Jordon into the Promised Land - and taught for over a year on all the aspects of the crossover.

I was excited to get the word, "After these things, I will bless you." In my heart I sincerely believed we were at the end of many things. The challenges were intense, and, finally, I felt we were coming up for air. We had had the wind of adversity blow over us for many years. Summing up the experiences in one word, it was "loss." We had lost so much in a variety of ways.

It was an already intense year. That May we hosted the 3D Woman Conference with Pastor Delia Knox. I leaned heavily on my eldest daughter, the Executive Pastor of the church. Because I was so exhausted, she stood in the gap, doing an outstanding job with the most minute details in everything.

In September of that same year Richard had a very bad fall, resulting in a serious back injury. His recovery was supernatural; so miraculous he is even stronger today. Then in December we lost our brother and Apostle David Keane. He went home to Jesus after an 8+ year illness. At that same time, I began to observe physical changes in my body. As Christmas and New Year's approached, the symptoms increased, and I went to see the doctor. The doctor recommended a colonoscopy as routine for a person my age.

At the first Sunday service of January 2015 Pastor Richard Keane declared "2015 The Year of the Word." We embarked in the new year with great expectations for open doors, even double open doors. Pastor Keane's exhortation to the whole church was the following: "It is not a famine of the Word in our ears, but a true response of obedience to the Word." Psalm 119: 133-136, *we must arise and see* what God sees. We have a task ahead of us and we must understand our mission.

John 8: 31-32, *If you abide in My Word, you are my disciples indeed and you shall know the truth, and the truth will make you free.* Jesus was speaking to those who believed in Him – Mighty Counselor, Prince of Peace. Agree with the Word. Mary had to agree, and we must agree that it is the Word that will make the difference.

We must believe what God has said. Repent and receive a renewing of the mind. Begin to think like Jesus, and revelation will come. Hold fast to My teaching and live in accordance to know, perceive, understand, and gain knowledge. This is knowledge that has an inception (a day when it was born) and has been revealed. This knowledge has a progression that leads to an attainment; the fullness of God in you.

This takes a renewing of the mind. When we recognize the truth, it affects our personal experience. The limitation of our minds says, "I cannot go through with this. I am not qualified. I can't speak." Jeremiah 1: 1-9 declares, *Behold, I have put My word in your mouth."* Touch my mouth with holy fire, and may every word I speak be your Word. God says He is ready to perform His Word, so arise and prepare yourself. No more delay. Prepare yourself and arise. God is making us resistant to the enemy; resistant to self-centeredness. He is moving us into a fortified "city" with an iron pillar. The enemy will fight against you, but they shall not prevail, for He is with us to deliver us.

Isn't God's love amazing? To think He would love me so much to send this Word at this time. He knows our name and our circumstance. He knows what we need

and sends it right on time. He knew what I was to face and how I would walk through it. He gave me a miracle before I knew I needed one. He sent me His Word, and by faith, I received and grew exponentially by it.

How do I know that the year was, indeed, the begining of my journey? In January, when the persisting symtoms emerged, we visited Richard's colleague for further investigation. The journey began with ultra sounds, blood tests, CT scan, and finally surgery. I was diagnosed with colon cancer. The date for surgery was set for 5th February 2015. It took 3 ½ hours. On that Thursday night the church stood in intercessory prayer for the duration. Apostle Franz Fletcher, along

with our very close friend Delroy Stennett, drove from Kingston simply to give support and prayer.

Surgery was successful, and, by the following Monday, I was home. So, the journey continued with chemotherapy and radiation for 7 weeks. The date is forever etched in my memory – 23rd March 2015 at 4:15 PM. Histology showed no organs or cells affected; no spread to the lymphatic system. Despite the good report, chemo and radiation were considered mandatory. I recall vividly the Sunday we told the church. A determined and absolute conviction of the word,

"God's Got This", rose up inside me. He really did because God had prepared us starting from the annivesary prophecy, "after these things, it's up from here!"

The year of the word, those words, The Word; they kept me. Jesus kept me! As I waited on the Lord, He spoke to me from John 9:31: *Now we know that God does not hear sinners, but if anyone is a worshipper of God and does his will, He hears him."* I got this! God's got this! This was the Word that I stood on, continuing to this day. Matthew 18:19 says *If two of you agree, it shall be done.* Richard and I agreed, and it was done. No cancer in my body.

Through the eyes of love, it pleased the Father to bruise Jesus. Jesus, in the Garden of Gethsemane, with vehement cries, asked His Father to let "this" cup pass. However, it pleased God the Father to bruise Him.

My Elizabeth was Mary.

Yes, that really is her name! She was touched with compassion for my feelings; spiritual synergy works miracles. She understood, through all my issues, wonderings, frustrations, and even doubts. She called each day before therapy, and she enquired again at the end of the day. Her endless prayers were raised with tremendous faith. She is an amazing woman of God, offering every morning for the duration of my journey an encouraging word, an enquiry, scripture, or song that helped me get up, stand, and continue standing.

"I sing because I am happy; I sing because I am free." "When I am down, and, oh, my soul so weary; when trouble comes, and my heart burdened be; then I am still and wait here in the silence until you come and sit awhile with me. You raise me up!" On March 26, 2015 I write in my journal: "I don't want to be here. I don't

want to feel the way I do. I want my life back. This treatment leaves me depressed," says my soul. "The enemy of my soul is on the attack. Oh, Lord, deliver me! I prophecy a relentless sword is coming down; a relentless spirit, never slacking, always pursuing, attacking, persistently pushing against the warfare over my soul.

Alas, I win!"

I declare this is the day the Lord has made, and I will be found by Him rejoicing in it. I can, to this day, hear David Keane, according to Isaiah 40, signing the words of this song: "Lord, you proved yourself to me. Your ways are not my ways, and your thoughts are not my thoughts. I want my life to be surrendered, Lord to thee, cause you proved yourself to me once more." When times of anxiety came along, diminishing my strength, the Lord was there to remind me that He cared about
every detail of my life. I know You, Lord, are always there cause you proved yourself to me.

During this epic battle for my soul, I had a visitation. I was sitting at my kitchentable deep in thoughts. I asked the Lord to touch me, to just simply let me know he was there with me. I told Him I had been reading and hearing about angelic visitations, and I wanted something to prove to me that I heard from Him. (John 9:31-33) "I GOT THIS." Suddenly, I felt the insulated, warm, comforting sense of a very large blanket wrapping me as a cocoon. "I GOT THIS." Overwhelmed with
confidence and peace that "every little thing was gonna be alright", I rose, went upstairs to our bedroom, sat in my usual place of meeting, and, with childlike wonder, whispered, "Lord, do it again." In quick response, that surreal, overwhelming touch of the wings of an angel enveloped me – holding me, healing me, filling me, strengthening me. I believed more than I ever had before; I understood what I knew even more. I had just experienced His tangible presence! The year of the Word! YES, indeed, it was going to be the year of the Word. It simply had to be! What did that mean to someone whose life had been changed forever? Three words cancelled the negative report – I GOT THIS!

I began a journey that helped me comprehend all the knowledge I had garnered over the years. This journey tested my understanding of self-talk and research,
recapping what I thought I had figured out about God. "Through it all, I learned to trust in Jesus. I learned to trust in God. Through it all, I learned to depend upon
His Word." According to Philippians 4:11 NKJV *For I have learned, in whatever state I am, to be content.* Philippians 4:13 TLB says, *For I can do everything God* asks me to with the help of Christ who gives me the strength and power.

Every day for six weeks, except for weekends that found me in family worship with the precious saints, I went to therapy. As we travelled along the path to Kingston, this song would play on the radio: "The road ahead is empty, it's paved with miles of the unknown." It became a challenge, even to this day, every time I heard it, but I have learned to trust in the Word. I have learned to stand in faith against that taunt that attempted to put efeat and hopelessness in my soul. My soul declared, "But the path of the just is like a shining sun that shines ever unto the perfect day. (Proverbs 4:18) I learned contentment, free from anxiety and worry, and independence from the enemy's lies. Sufficiency and satisfaction came to me from the only place it can; the presence of God.

On this journey, I also engaged in a state of mind where my desires were confined to my lot for the season. This opposed the ambitions of the devil to inflict fear and
doubt. For God was in the midst, and it was His might, not by my might; not by my power; but completely by His Spirit. There arose an inward disposition that, I was
told later, was the offspring of humility. I could not do one thing to change my situation, but Jesus could, and can!

I began to enjoy the greatness of divine promises and provision. Because the Spirit supplied satisfaction with what I had, what I received was simply enough to take care of my every need. GOD'S GOT THIS. I was content with Jesus' dealing in my affairs because I knew He was working all things for my good. Moreover, amid even unfavourable circumstances, He was perfecting the things that concerned me.

I began to feel an inward satisfaction and fulfilment. I became reasonably happy and satisfied with the way things were, having to relocate to another city for
treatment, leaving family and loved ones and going into what seemed a giant unknown. However, leaving behind all that made for my peace, I accepted my lot
rather than taking further actions in my own strength or making demands of others. I was certain about my welfare; GOD'S GOT THIS. He is intentional about my destiny, and I am fine with that!

Chapter 9. The Sounding of Mary's Worship

"The Lord gave a word; great was the company of women who proclaimed it" Psalm 68:11

The sound of Mary's worship exhaled from her deepest emotions, alive with passion and zeal for God's presence and God Himself. Regardless of our situation,
as God's child, we may clothe and carry ourselves with strength and dignity. This attire is available to us by God's great grace. Psalm 26:8 says "Lord, I have loved
the habitation of your house and the place of your glory." Mary's first step was accepting the Word of God humbly, recognizing Him as Lord. Mary was already
developed in the knowledge of the Word. We must do the same. We are developed spiritually by the Word, and in the presence of God, you will hear His voice and be obedient.

John 4:23 quotes Jesus: "God is seeking true worshippers; those who worship Him in spirit and in truth." Pastor Sharon Wooten of Real-Life Ministries wrote a song: "Here's my worship; take joy in it; make it your dwelling place. I wanna put a smile on Your Face. I present my heart to You... Here's my worship...Smile, Here's my heart... Smile, Here's my life.. Smile.
We cooperate with the Holy Spirit and walk in the fruit that it bears. Learn the daily discipline of submitting to the lordship of

Jesus Christ, regardless of personal
emotions or circumstances of life. Cultivate a righteous consciousness instead of a sinful consciousness. Know this from now
on – we are warriors who have a mind
set on God, giving no place to the enemy. We walk and live by
faith. We speak faith-filled words. Be givers without hesitation,
reluctance, or resistance.

Warriors are extravagant in their worship. They never come
empty-handed and always have a praise. Warriors cannot be
bought nor go unnoticed. They are obedient to the Spirit because
of a deep hunger to know the ways of God. As Jesus says in John
4:23, *God is seeking true worshippers; those who worship Him* in
spirit and in truth.

Mary's Song

Mary released a sound into the atmosphere that not only connected with heaven, but opened its portals, giving heaven authority to invoke and manifest the rights of the Kingdom. Mary, by
her praise, openly exercised a right for heavenly influence on the
earth. Her praise opened the portals of heaven and kept them
open for the released angelic activity. Her praise ascended into
the atmosphere with authority and declarations that could be
confirmed by heaven. Her praise
sent a warning to the kingdom of darkness – The King is here!

Luke 1:46 says *My soul magnifies the Lord and my spirit has rejoiced
in God my Savior.* Mary declared "my soul", owning the part that
is capable of feeling and perception. The soul is that part of man
that can respond emotionally, rather than intellectually. It is the

element of created man by which he perceives, reflects, feels, and desires. It is the seat of will and purpose; the seat of appetite.

"My soul magnifies..." spoken by a true woman who willingly reflected beauty and the heart of God to her world. Mary had a life surrendered in total abandonment to God; she was sold out. She lived a life seeking to be Godcentered, trusting Him, and saying, "Yes, Lord, be it unto me according to your Word." She had a feminine heart filled with purpose mandated to a nation. Her heart, at that moment, had the greatness of all possibilities on the inside of her.

Her song is a reflection of God's own heart. Mary was a woman to the very core of her being, singing a magnificent song, speaking out for an amazing, supernatural, overwhelming in-filling until she radiated the fullness of God. The move of the Holy Spirit had taken control of her being; she called Him Lord and acknowledged Him as her Savior.

What a worship that exuded from one who considered herself ordinary and lowly. Mary praised God, not only for using her, but for the realization of the purpose
for which she was being called. She worshipped Him for His mercy towards His beloved Israel. Mary remembered she carried the Messiah, the Savior of the world, the Reconciler, Emmanuel, God with us. She was chosen to give birth to the answer for deliverance, peace, justice, and everlasting life. Oh, how her spirit, and mine too, rejoices in God my Savior.

Her Spirit

What is the spirit? The life principle bestowed on man by God; the force of a person characterizing a life - being; the immaterial, powerful, invisible part of man that speaks to moral qualities and activities and that rejoices in God. The new wine had come to Mary with a refreshing flood. Her joy could not be contained, for in her womb she carried the very seed of God.

We develop a passion for God through the heart of true worship; heart to heart. Psalm 84: 1-10 tells us King David's heart longed for this as he engaged his soul to
worship God. He spoke of how his soul panted and yearned after the courts of the Lord. David's heart and his flesh hungered for the presence of the Lord so much that he envied the sparrow.

When, like Mary, we have the revelation that we carry in us the seed of God, Jesus the Word, we will not be contained, nor will we keep silent. We carry in us
resurrection power, born of the spirit, the Kingdom of God. We will learn how to engage in praise and allow ourselves to flow into spontaneous worship by cultivating an appetite for more of God. We will have this insatiable thirst for the Living God, not being simply satisfied with someone else's worship. Rather than
just singing words that sound good, we will step into the zone of yourself and God alone.

Therefore, we no longer must wait to go to church or wait for the music to begin for worship time for worship to ooze out of us. My voice, my words, my emotions, my shout, my worship causes true worshippers to worship without faking it. My worship emerges as I absorb myself in the Word, especially the Gospels, where
we get to know Jesus; who He was, what He said, and the ministry He performed.

I acknowledge and learn about His authority. Becoming a worshipper in spirit and truth comes straight from the heart. This is where God looks first; a broken spirit
and a contrite heart, He will not reject.

The Heart

The heart is the seat of affection, ambition, passion, and appetite. It controls the will and actions of the innermost center of the natural condition of man. The
heart is the center of social life and the reservoir of the entire life power. It includes intellect, as well as affections and will. Our heart and head (mind) act and
react to one another.

Our heart issues are important to God. He wants us to have peaceful hearts that can enjoy fellowship; a fellowship that strengthens the heart that leads to the
strengthening of the whole man. The heart of man is the center of the rational and spiritual condition of man. Worship and the heart are inseparable since the
heart is the receptacle of God's love and the in-dwelling place of Christ in us. It is the seat of love and hate, and the heart knows understands, and reflects.
The heart is also the center of feelings, joy, acceptance, rejection, and pain. The heart is where deliverance takes place first. The heart is the dwelling place of the
Holy Spirit where the peace of God abides. The heart is the closet of secret communion with God. Our hearts are like a garden, so our part is to be watchful of anything that may threaten them. "If I regard iniquity in my heart, the Lord will not hear me." (Psalm 66:18) "Tending" the garden of our hearts is the same way
Adam was commanded to tend the Garden of Eden.
It means to place a hedge of protection; to be circumspect, take heed, look narrowly, observe; to preserve,
regard, save, watch, and discern.

God has commanded us to tend our hearts. How do I keep my

heart in Eden? The following are the guards we should have: an exercise of the fruit of the Spirit, the

Word, and of prayer; Trust and acknowledgment of the Lord at all times, not leaning on our own understanding. God delights in the heart and the lifestyle of worshippers. Nothing pleases Him more than the quality of life displayed by a worshipper. We cooperate with the Holy Spirit and walk in the subsequent fruit.

The fruit of the Holy Spirit will always keep our hearts in the love of Jesus Christ. Learn the daily discipline of submitting to the Lordship of Jesus Christ, regardless

of personal emotions or the circumstances of life. Cultivate a righteous consciousness, instead of a sinful consciousness. We are warriors with a mind set on God, allowing no place to the enemy. Walk and live by faith; speak faith-filled words. Warriors are givers without hesitation, reluctance or resistance. Warriors are extravagant in their worship, never coming empty-handed and always having a praise. They cannot be bought or go unnoticed. True worshippers are obedient

to the Spirit because of a deep hunger to know the ways of God. A new order of priesthood has been raised up through the ultimate sacrifice of the Messiah, Jesus Christ, the Anointed One, the only Spotless Lamb. Man is physical, emotional, and spiritual with his basic needs. God created us with an innate desire to love and to be loved, as well as with a passion to worship. When

man seeks to meet his own needs, he becomes driven in his attempts for satisfaction. However, he seeks created things rather than the Creator for that satisfaction. The way a man perceives himself, his world, and God will determine how he will behave and respond. Our environment and our relationship with God will determine what and who we become.

It is the spirit of man that connects with God and cries out, through his emotions, for change. However, it is through the

Spirit that we experience the presence of
God. Psalm 84: 1-10 shares how developing a passion for God is
the heart of true worship. King David had a passion for God's presence and a zeal for His house. He
spoke of how his soul pants and yearns after the courts of the
Lord. His heart and his flesh hungered for the presence of the Lord
so much he envied the sparrow.
Engage in praise and allow yourself to flow into spontaneous
worship. True worshippers will worship; you can't fake it. Absorb
yourself in the Word, especially the Gospels, and get to know
Jesus; who He was, what He said, and the ministry He did on
earth. Acknowledge and learn about His authority. Becoming a
worshipper in spirit and in truth comes straight from the heart.
This is where God looks first. A broken spirit and a contrite heart
He will not reject. God delights in the lifestyle of worshippers.
Nothing please Him more than the quality of life displayed by a
worshipper. (Matthew 13:3)

We have a heart destination, and its path has already been charted
by the Lord for us from the foundation of the earth. We know the
Word says, "Without faith,
it is impossible to please god", but the vehicle is the heart. David
was a man after God's own heart. He worshipped God with the
knowledge of who God is and with the revelation of God's sovereignty. If you have a heart of a worshipper, the Lord is searching
for you. The heart of a worshipper knows how to disentangle and
will not remain encumbered by cares. God expects us to be obedient and guard our hearts as He instructed Mary, for out of the
heart flows the issues of life.
Out of the abundance of the heart the mouth speaks. The mouth,
with its corresponding words, equals life or death. A heart that
is hardened by circumstances cannot receive the Word; it becomes impenetrable. A heart that has had an experience with God
but has found no depth and has not been nurtured, protected or

guarded, gets scorched by the enemy's fiery darts. The heart withers because it had no watering of the Word.

A heart that cares, but is choked by the stranglehold of emotions, will not receive healing by the Living Word. This heart vessel will find it difficult to submit; however, it an be delivered by the love of God in worship. It can be transformed into a yielded vessel with a soul that magnifies the Lord and with a spirit that cannot be contained. God is in the house as a vessel available to be used as desired by Him. This heart is the container prepared for the secrets and mysteries of the kingdom of heaven. Precious treasures in earthen vessels might be

troubled and oppressed in every way, but they are not trampled. This vessel has the resurrection life of Jesus resident in our mortal bodies.

True Worshippers Will Worship

God delights in the lifestyle of worshippers. Nothing please Him more than the quality displayed by a worshipper. A worshipper is someone who has learned the

daily discipline of submitting to the Lordship of Christ regardless of personal and emotional circumstances in life. (II Corinthians 10: 4-6) We know from Jesus' declaration who the Father is seeking. The Father is seeking worshippers. He is always seeking those who have adopted the lifestyle and mindset of worship. We can see the Samaritan woman in John 4:23 and the woman with the alabaster box in Luke 7: 36-50. This account of the woman with the alabaster box is one of the most profound postures of a true worshipper. In this account, Jesus reveals both the secrets and the rewards of worship.

Worshippers experience the forgiveness of sin. They are warriors and have their minds set on God. Worshippers do not allow room for distraction, and they walk

by faith, not by sight. They are givers with no hesitation, no reluctance, no resistance, not grudgingly. Worshippers are extravagant in worship and in their
love for God. They walk in obedience and the fear of the Lord. They are understanding of God's ways and His character and desire to please Him.
Worshippers never come empty-handed. (Psalm 96: 8-9) Worshippers are sincere and will not go unnoticed.

Restore Holy Altars Of Worship

Isaiah 58

We preach to the symptoms of things rather than to the roots, and worship is at the root for an inside-out experience. Often, we get caught up in the expressions
of worship, so worship becomes the program rather than the heart of worship.
What is your heart song? In Amos 5:21 God had rejected their worship, and they did not even know it. Unless your worship is aligned, you cannot worship in spirit and truth. *Psalm 139:13-14 says For You created my inmost being; you knit me together in my mother's womb. I praise You because I am fearfully and wonderfully made.*

The next insurgence of what God is going to do is in performing arts. Prophetic worship and dance have a great effect on worship, as does creativity in art and
paintings, etc. However, only a seeker of truth will please God. You never have to perform for God. Our salvation is not based on our talents. Hebrews 10:16 says *I will put my law in their hearts and I will write them on their minds.*

Romans 12: 2 tells to not conform. Do a heart check on your-self. Brokenness and tears are truly key elements of worship. The woman with the alabaster box was broken and allowed her fra-grance to rise. (Psalm 51:17, Isaiah 57:15, Isaiah 66: 1-2) *The sac-rifice of God is a broken spirit, a broken and a contrite heart. These, O God, you will not despise.* Worship is the posture of the heart.

Posture means to act in an affected or artificial manner, as to create a certain impression. Worship is usually intimate. Worship may not always be evident to an observer. It is primarily a verti-cal interaction of private preoccupation with the Godhead. Wor-ship is not a musical activity necessarily, but a function of the heart. It is a spontaneous yielding to the will of God and respond-ing to His love.

Worship is sensitivity to His presence, not to the human efforts of others. Bowing, kneeling, and laying prostrate do not necessarily mean they are in worship.

Worship is basking in God's presence and acknowledging Him for who He is.

"Lord, I praise you because of who You are." How do I know He is here? Matthew 18:20 tells us *where two or three are gathered together in My name, I am there in the midst of them.* In the gathering, the two or three must be in unity. (at least two for an agreement to be legal) Also in the gathering, it must be in His name.

Our spirit is willing to worship, and it is simply a matter of un-locking your spirit. How do I do this? I unlock my spirit by yield-ing my thoughts and mind to the activity of the Holy Spirit. I submit my human spirit to the Holy Spirit. We reject the mindset leading us away from the flow of the Holy Spirit: How do I look? How do I sound? This is stupid. I don't need to do this. I submit my attitude, imagination and reasoning to The Holy Spirit.

Watch your posture and your surroundings. Are you embarrassed or ashamed of Jesus? Worship is an experience and a learned behavior. Psalm 89: 15 tells us it is an art of expressing oneself to God. Like prayer, worship is learned by engaging in it. In worship we must be led by the Spirit, for the Spirit knows the mind of the Father. (Romans 8)

The true worshippers cannot go un-noticed, for they will attract attention by worship's fluid beauty, even, in some eyes, extravagant. Because some do not want to attract attention, they have resisted entering into the fullness of worship.
They are afraid of what others may think of them! Peer pressure does affect worship. It has held back countless precious saints from the blessing of opening their hearts to the Lord.

True worship will invoke the criticism of the spiritually barren, but the true worshippers are willing to pay the price regardless. There are no formulas for
worship, because worship is a function of the heart. The heart will find expression in a variety of external forms. As a river of God begins to flow during our times of worship, it will bring life, abundance, and healing. It will wash over broken hearts and will restore parched souls. However, It is possible for us to come to a good
understanding of worship's dynamics without ever making an application to our lives.

It is one thing to know what worship is. It is quite another thing to become a true worshipper. Worship is love responding to Love; spirit to spirit; while praise is
outward. Worship is both an inward and an outward expression. Expressions like kneeling, lying prostrate before God, singing heartfelt feelings of love, words of
adoration, pouring out inner affections, devotion, and commit-

ment.

A worshipper does not come with a beggar's mentality. Why? We are heirs and joint heirs with Jesus. We have been engrafted into the body by the Spirit of Adoption. We cry, Abba, Father. We are the righteousness of God by the blood covenant. We can enter boldly into the throne of grace because we are children, not orphans.

The Sounding Of Worship

The sounding of worship is not its harmony, but the measurement of the depth. (Delia Knox) Acts 27:28 tells us they took soundings and found the water was only 120 fathoms. They took the soundings again and found it to be fifty fathoms.

Elizabeth's baby leaped in her womb at the sound of Mary's greeting. (Luke 1:44) For indeed, as soon as the voice of your greeting sounded in my ear, the babe
leaped in my womb for joy.

We keep the sounding of our worship constant. It is so easy to get off course or distracted. A deeper dimension comes from a worshipper whose only desire is to
know more of the character of the one worshipped. The worshipper wants and longs for more of the object of our worship. Beyond our five senses, worship is more than words. The sounding of our worship is deep calling unto the depth not reached by human efforts. The sounding of worship goes further and moves boundaries, going beyond limits of time and space.

The sounding of our worship is when we seek to step from our limitations to the knowledge of third dimension worship; Father, Son, and Holy Spirit presence of
God, where the glory is. Ezekiel 47: 1-4 gives a phenomenal account of the sounding of our worship: *water running out of the*

right side of the Spirit of the Lord. The position of the ankle, the knee, and the waist represent a different sounding. Ezekiel 47:5 says *He measured one thousand, and it was a river that I* could not cross for the water was too deep, water in which one must swim, a river that could not be crossed.

The Purpose Of Our Worship

To be consumed by the Holy Spirit exudes the power of God. This power is for the purpose of healing and deliverance in this end time harvest. We will bear fruit.
Ezekiel 47: 12 confirms this, *along the bank of the river, on this side and that, will* grow all kinds of trees used for food. Their leaves will not whither, and its fruits will not fail. They will bear fruit every month because their water flows from the sanctuary. Their fruit will be for food and their leaves for medicine.

This speaks to the supernatural move of God as His worshippers, who seek after the Spirit and for truth, come into a fresh revelation of God's divine will and purpose for the harvest. The food and medicine for God's people is found in our worship and the Word. God is preparing an army of trusted saints whom he can trust with His anointing to gather this harvest for the kingdom of heaven.

Mary's worship was consistent, held together by the power and promises in the Word. Colossians 1: 17 *He was before all else began and it is His power that holds*
everything together. Mary's worship was pure, held together simply by the integrity of the object of her worship and the infallible Word of God. Mary's worship was one of her highest virtues. Engaging discernment of the power of the lie of the enemy, she was free to rely upon the wise counsel and the character of the God both feared and loved. Her spirit of worship was excellent,

reasonable, and logically harmonious. She was able to maintain a particular standard with respect.

Her worship said, "Lord, I can trust You." Mary's worship, while ver strong and convincing, had a positive influence, but not controlling! Her heart's cry was sensitive, but not needy; this young virgin had a healthy self-image. Her worship came out of the fear of God and enabled her to make a decision; she would not allow her earthly state to dictate her self-esteem, but she would release herself into the identity gifted by God. Henceforth, she would forever be known as Mary, the mother of Jesus of Nazareth, the Messiah, the Savior of the World.

Mary's posture before the Lord has distinguished her among women as a vessel of honor, in prudence and dignity. The virtue and humility in her conduct was
pleasing to God and has left an ever living example attainable for all who would choose to worship in a spirit that is real. Our worship must engage our spirit in the pursuit of the true and living God. As the deer pants after the water, so we must search and thirst for God.

We who are called worshippers come simply and honestly, withholding nothing, bringing our all. We worship out of our very being in adoration, casting our
earthly crown, crying holy.

About the Author

Dr. Karene Joye Keane (DCC)

Dr. K. Joye Keane was born in Montego Bay Jamaica and has lived there to date. She however, has travelled internationally both as a love for travel as well as to minister the word of God.

She is a graduate of Montego Bay High School and has pursued studies in Ministerial and Christian counseling. She received her Doctorate in Christian Counseling (DCC) in 2008, from Central Christian University, North Carolina USA, and is a licensed member of the National Christian Counselors Association (NCCA) since 2001. Dr. Keane was ordained to ministry in November 1999 by the laying on of hands by the Presbytery under the leadership of Apostle David Keane.

On 12 August 2018 she was set in as Senior Pastor as her husband Dr. Richard Keane received the mantels of Apostle of Family Church on the Rock Montego Bay and Negril.

In that same year she was invited to serve on the Board of Management of The Herbert Morrison Technical High School in Montego Bay.

Pastor Joye presents the truth of God's word in her way that is powerful, passionate, personal and prophetic. Being called by God to His ministry, the anointing on her life is evident in all that she does. Her gifting as a psalmist became evident as she pioneered the Praise and Worship ministry of Family Church on the Rock over the past thirty (30) years; she leads the people into a dimension of worship to our Lord Jesus Christ and teaches how to access the throne room of God. She has also written and recorded songs and written 2 devotionals "Unspeakable Joy" and "Voices of Many Waters" – all exhibiting her poetic gifting and demonstrating her desire for God's presence to touch the lives of others.

As the visionary of "Women in Fellowship and Ministry" (WIFAM), she has a heart for training the next generation and raising up women of excellence. Her commitment to empower women in their sense of worth and leadership is demonstrated by the teaching and ministry of the very principles that Jesus taught.

Being submitted to the vision of Family Church OnThe Rock in Isaiah 61, her insight has guided many through her teaching programs and continues to develop leaders through weekly training, ongoing encounters and "Prayer Covenant Connector (PCC) teachings" have helped steer the direction of FCOTR and challenges the lives of those who have sat under her ministry.

K. Joye Keane having a great sense of family is a great householder, loves cooking, baking and decorating among many other talents. She is married to Richard Mark Keane, a Medical Doctor and Justice of the Peace for 40 years, has three (3) adult girls and four (4) grandchildren.

Made in the USA
Middletown, DE
24 April 2021

38382323R10066